LOWE'S
Improving Home Improvement

creative
ideas
for KIDS' SPACES

LOWE'S COMPANIES, INC.

Robert Niblock, CEO AND
   CHAIRMAN OF THE BOARD

Larry D. Stone, PRESIDENT

Melissa S. Birdsong,
   VP, TREND, DESIGN & BRAND

Sarah Wagner, MERCHANDISING DIRECTOR

Bob Gfeller, SENIOR VP, MARKETING

Pete Woods, VP, ADVERTISING

Carol Knuth, VP, MERCHANDISING

Nick Canter, EXECUTIVE VP, MERCHANDISING

Sandy Culver,
   CUSTOMER RELATIONSHIP MANAGER

LOWE'S CREATIVE IDEAS FOR KIDS' SPACES

René Klein,
   PROJECT DIRECTOR FOR LOWE'S CUSTOM BOOKS,
   SUNSET PUBLISHING CORPORATION

Stephanie Patton,
   DIRECTOR, SPC CUSTOM PUBLISHING

Christina Lynch,
   ACCOUNT MANAGER, SPC CUSTOM PUBLISHING

Alice Lankford Elmore, EDITOR

Josh Garskof, WRITER

Sally W. Smith, CONSULTING EDITOR

Jennifer Allen, ART DIRECTOR

Amy R. Bickell, DESIGNER

Robin Miller, ILLUSTRATOR

Shelley DeLuca, COPY CHIEF

Amanda Kuhnert and Dawn Russell, COPY EDITORS

Sheryl Jones, PRODUCTION MANAGER

Chambliss Keith, PRODUCTION ASSISTANT

Nanette Cardon, INDEXER

Ashley Arthur, Laurie C. Kilpatrick, Molly J. Rogers,
CONTRIBUTORS

Cover: Durable finishes and kid-friendly surfaces coexist
with cheerful colors and classic design in this child's
space. The room's worry-free nature makes it perfect for
parents seeking low-maintenance shortcuts and for kids
looking to unleash their creativity.

Photograph: Bryan Johnson

10 9 8 7 6 5 4 3

First Printing January 2005

For additional copies of *Creative Ideas for Kids' Spaces*
or any other Lowe's book, visit
www.sunsetbooks.com or call 1-800-526-5111.

PHOTO CREDITS:

Left (L), Center (C), Right (R), Top (T), Middle (M), Bottom (B)

Jean Allsopp: 11BC, 19TL, 21BR, 24BL, 34TR, 36TL, 56TR, 61BL; Robbie Caponetto:
100TR, 112TL, 116BL; Van Chaplin: 27BR, 54TC, 63TR, 74TL, 80BL, 80TR, 82BL,
99BL, 106TR, 118BL, 118TR, 124TR, 125BL; ClosetMaid: 27TC, 29TR; William
Dickey: 117TR; Getty Images: 7BL, 14BR; Laurey W. Glenn: 8TR, 12BL, 16BL, 22TR,
24TL, 26TR, 26BR, 31TL, 32BR, 33TL, 43TR, 46TR, 48TR, 49BL, 58BL, 70TR,
70BR, 71TL, 78TR, 82TL, 88TL, 93TR, 96TR, 105TL, 105TR, 122BL, 122TR; David
Hill: 86BL, 86TR; Bryan Johnson: 6TL, 41TL, 55MR, 64ML, 64BR, 69TL, 72TC,
72BL, 79TR, 83TR, 98TR, 99TR, 99MR, 99BR, 101TR, 120TL, 120BL, 120TR;
Muffey Kibbey: 10TR, 38BR, 39BL; Sylvia Martin: 8BL, 18TL, 18BL, 21TL, 22BL,
32TR, 32MR, 51ML, 65TR; National Geographic: 121TR, 121BR; John O'Hagan:
17TR, 17BR, 20TR, 25TL, 28TL, 28BL, 28TR, 30TL, 30TR, 30BR, 32BL, 34BR,
37ML, 37BR, 38TL, 39MR, 40TR, 40BR, 42TL, 43ML, 45BR, 50TR, 51TR, 52TR,
55TR, 55MR, 56MR, 59TR, 60TR, 60BR, 61ML, 62TL, 62BR, 63BL, 64MR, 64BR,
66TL, 66BL, 67BR, 68TL, 68BL, 69BL, 69BR, 76TR, 84TR, 85BL, 85TR, 88BL,
88TR, 90TL, 92TL, 92TR, 93BR, 94ML, 94BL, 94TR, 94BR, 95BL, 95TR, 102BL,
102TR, 104TL, 108TL, 110BL, 110TR, 111BR, 114TR, 115TL, 115ML, 115BL,
125TL; Chris Padgett: 36TL; Meg McKinney: 14TL, 45TR; Bruce Wagman: 98BR

bring your ideas
to life...

Whether you have **children** of your own or children that you love to call your own, you realize what a **joy** they can be. And when they live or spend a lot of time in your home, you also know that children can change your perspective on **decorating and organizing.** We want to **help** you transform a room or your entire home into a space that is kid-friendly and **stylish.** That's why we've brought you this book, filled with innovative **ideas** and informative **advice** that will help you in your quest to create a nursery, a kid-proof backyard, or perhaps just some toy storage in your family room.

You also will notice **projects** on all levels throughout the book that will show you how to add some flair to your **child's spaces.** Each comes with a shopping list of items from Lowe's. These ideas, as well as the wealth of photographs we've included, will **inspire you**—and your children, if they're old enough—to bring new life to a space they use frequently.

Finally, we want to introduce you (or reintroduce you) to our *Lowe's Creative Ideas* book series. The first two installments, *Lowe's Creative Ideas for Outdoor Living* and *Lowe's Creative Ideas for Organizing Your Home,* can be purchased at your local Lowe's store along with books from Lowe's other series, which includes the recent *Lowe's Complete Tile & Flooring.* You'll **discover** that they're filled with the same type of clever ideas and **practical information** that you'll find in the pages of our magazine, *Lowe's Creative Ideas.*

p.s.

Melissa

Melissa Birdsong
Director, Trend and Design
Lowe's Companies, Inc.

72

112

contents

LowesCreativeIdeas.com

6 KIDS' BEDROOMS

8 Infants and Toddlers

12 Young Children

16 Older Children

18 Shared Bedrooms

22 Adapting as the Child Grows

24 Bedroom Storage

28 Storing Clothing

32 Collectibles and Displays

34 Room for Play, Study, and Hobbies

38 Walls

42 Flooring

44 Furniture

48 Accessories

52 KIDS' BATHROOMS

54 Planning the Space

56 Simple Renovations

60 Shared Spaces

64 Easy Use and Accessibility

66 Storage

70 Accessories

74 AROUND THE HOUSE

76 Planning the Space
80 Family Rooms
86 Playrooms
96 Kitchens

100 Controlling
 Entryway Clutter
102 Storage

108 OUTDOOR SPACES

110 Planning the Space
116 Storage

118 Kids' Gardens
124 Fences

126 Index
128 At Lowe's . . . We're Here for You!

kids' bedroom

WHAT A GREAT IDEA

PAGE 40 FOLLOW OUR STEP-BY-STEP
INSTRUCTIONS TO CREATE THIS VIBRANT PAINT
TREATMENT IN YOUR CHILD'S BEDROOM.

SETTING UP A CHILD'S BEDROOM can be an exciting and emotional project. After all, many formative hours will be spent in this space: Your child may take his first steps on the carpet you select, read his first words while sitting on the bed, or learn to play a musical instrument in the overstuffed chair. More than anything, you want the room to be safe, comfortable, and inspiring.

Some parents vividly envision the final product. For example, you may dream of a classic baby blue or powder pink color scheme, or perhaps a more dramatic multitiered loft space. You may want to re-create your childhood room—or to design the room that you always wished for while you were growing up. But in many instances, parents are still searching for just the right theme. If you're one of those, you probably are looking for a place to get started.

Take a deep breath. The following pages are filled with great ideas and simple guidelines for creating an environment that fosters growth and exploration. You'll learn everything from the moods evoked by certain color palettes to the best ways to accommodate growing kids. We even explain how particular decorating choices can help to improve your child's study habits, encourage him to clean up his room, and stimulate his artistic talents.

LEFT: Playful horizontal stripes in bright green and blue seem to expand this bedroom. The interesting wall design can be produced using paint, tape, and a level.

infants and toddlers

AS MUCH FUN AS IT IS TO CREATE A NURSERY, the reality is that infants aren't able to appreciate much beyond simple shapes and colors. A baby needs a crib, a changing station, and an overall safe environment (see the Safety Checklist on page 11 for more information). Beyond these features, the nursery is really more for the parents, who will spend many hours in the room.

There should be no rush to complete the nursery before the baby is born. For the first few months, infants often sleep in a bassinet in their parents' room. The nursery becomes a necessity once your little one graduates to the crib. If you design the room after the baby arrives you will know the baby's gender and be aware of your needs as new parents, thus enabling you to organize the space efficiently.

A BASIC START The crib typically is the first item on the list of must-have nursery furnishings, but consider additional pieces to ease your life as a new parent. A rocking chair with a footstool makes feedings and story time easier. You certainly will want efficient storage for diaper-changing essentials: Place a caddy or shelves within arm's reach of the changing station. Keep in mind that a dedicated changing table isn't required; if space is tight, attach a pad to the top of a dresser or desk for this purpose.

ABOVE: A mobile over the crib provides visual stimulation. The chest of drawers serves as a changing table with storage for necessities.

BRIGHT EYES

YOU'LL WANT TO EQUIP THE ROOM with a few activities and stimulating items to attract your baby's attention as his eyesight improves. Try these fun tips.

• Hang melodic, colorful mobiles above the changing station and crib.

• Fill a basket with stuffed animals, rattles, and books.

• Attach a baby-safe plastic mirror to the inside of the crib so that your baby can spend time enjoying his own cute little baby face.

LEFT: Purple walls combine with accents of blue, green, and citrus hues for a playful palette.

young children

BY THE AGE OF 3, a child has developed a strong sense of his likes and dislikes—and plenty of opinions about how his bedroom should be decorated. At this point, it is important to involve him in the planning. The best approach may be for you to control the options available to him, thus keeping them manageable, and then act as the final word. This way you will ensure his room is filled with items he loves that are also safe and long-lasting.

MAKING CHOICES EASY Since you can't exactly give a 3-year-old total decorating control, shopping together could be a frustrating experience for everyone involved. And because youngsters usually don't have the stamina for browsing, they frequently are attracted to impractical or inappropriate items.

For these reasons, consider selecting a few options yourself and presenting them to your child. Wall colors are fun to pick when you're playing with paint chips and wallpaper samples. Furniture, light fixtures, and accessories can be chosen from catalog clippings or Web site printouts. Or make the process even simpler with themed coordinates in linens, wallcoverings, and hardware from Lowe's.

LASTING STYLE While the bedroom your young child helped decorate may not appeal to him once he reaches age 10 or 12, you can keep the room from instantly looking dated by choosing items that are adaptable as the child grows. You will get the longest life out of items in your youngster's room if you select classic styles and colors. Wood and metal finishes last for decades. Paint unfinished pieces in a neutral shade or repaint as tastes change.

ABOVE: An elegant iron bed will make a smooth transition to a guestroom if your daughter ever tires of it.

A storybook-inspired mural adorns one wall in this sweetly fashioned bedroom.

Any young cowboy will get a kick out of this Western-themed bedroom. Accessories and "brands" stamped on the wall can be changed easily when he reaches his teen years.

GETTING A GOOD FIT

Before buying any furniture, quickly draw a floor plan by roughly sketching the shape of the room as if you were observing it from the ceiling. Next, measure the walls and note the dimensions on the sketch. Also measure and mark all doors, windows, radiators, and other obstructions on the sketch. Finally, you may want to add the room's activity zones, such as play, sleep, reading, and craft areas. Take the sketch and a tape measure on all of your shopping trips. Measure any furniture you plan to buy, and check the dimensions against your sketch to determine whether it's a good fit.

fit to a "t"

AS YOU DESIGN YOUR CHILD'S SPACE, ORIENT IT TO HIS HEIGHT AND EYE LEVEL.

A typical 3-year-old has an eye level of 33 inches high, and he can reach as high as 41 inches. A 5-year-old usually has a 35- to 43-inch eye level and can reach up to 43 to 52 inches. And the average 9-year-old has a 43- to 53-inch eye level and can reach 53 to 65 inches high. Keep those numbers in mind— or measure your child to come up with more specific figures—as you arrange shelving, work surfaces, and interesting wall displays.

Ideal Shelving Dimensions for Children

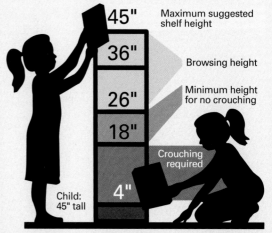

45" — Maximum suggested shelf height

36" — Browsing height

26" — Minimum height for no crouching

18"

Crouching required

4"

Child: 45" tall

older children

PRETEENS AND TEENS tend to take their rooms pretty seriously. They become self-conscious if the decor seems babyish or uncool, and they are likely to spearhead a complete makeover if given the opportunity. Hopefully they'll discuss their plans with you first so you can agree on a design or theme.

The preteen years are the perfect time to reconfigure toy-storage areas to make space for clothing, CDs, computers, and other items that now interest your child. A desk for studying without distraction also should be included in the room.

As youthful accessories and artwork are removed or replaced, take the opportunity to explore new decorating ideas that are appealing to both you and your child. A great place to start is by choosing a new color palette. Take her to Lowe's to look at paint chips for repainting the bedroom—or the furniture—and be sure to allow her to share her preferences and make some of the decisions herself. Check out the in-store literature on exciting color combinations and interesting faux finishes. Then tackle the project as a team.

OPPOSITE PAGE: Red dominates in this "wild" bedroom. A variety of fabrics creates a colorful, but decidedly preteen, atmosphere.
BELOW: A favorite sports team's colors inspired the palette for this boy's room.

BELOW: Trendy linens, oversized accessories, and a paper lantern add striking style to an otherwise simple room. A soft backdrop of fabric hangs from drawer pulls on the wall behind the bed.

SHARED BEDROOMS work best for children who are separated by 3 to 5 years in age. Competition often arises when there is less of a difference, while a lack of shared interests can be a problem for those separated by many years. Same-gender siblings are most successful as roommates because their interests and activities are more likely to mesh.

Provide a communal space in the room where the children can play together, as well as personal spaces where they can find time alone. For youngsters, personal space need not be very private. Each child may prefer to have his own bed, desk, chest of drawers, and a few personal toys and belongings. But as the teen years approach, real privacy is needed, and that takes some decorating finesse.

Start by creating sleeping quarters that are as equally divided as possible. However, few rooms will allow for

Here, equal and similar spaces were created for the siblings sharing this room. A trundle under each bed offers space for guests and can be tucked away when not in use.

In this room, each child has her own bed and artwork. The styles of the beds are not an exact match, yet their pine construction provides a unifying element.

The design of this bedroom allows each child to have her own window. Private sleeping spaces are separated by a shared desk.

ABOVE: Clean lines and simple decor keep this shared attic space from seeming cluttered or cramped.

STACKED BEDS PROVIDE AN EXCELLENT WAY TO CONSERVE SPACE IN A SHARED BEDROOM WHILE ALSO GIVING EACH CHILD SOME PRIVACY.

• **Buy units that will separate** into individual twin beds so that when the kids outgrow the bunk-bed phase you can arrange them in a new way.

• **The upper bunk should have sturdy guard rails** on any edge that's not against a wall and an attached ladder that's easy for your child to climb.

• **Don't put anyone under 6** years old in the upper bunk.

• **Make sure there's space for each child** to sit up in bed—with growing room to spare.

• **Reading lights near each bed** will supply good task lighting. Consider installing a wall sconce or a clip-on lamp (with an onboard switch in either case) above the headboard.

perfectly identical sides with matching windows and square footage, so compromise will be required. If one child's area includes a window, then perhaps the other is compensated with a little extra space. Or if one has the closet, maybe the other gets an armoire.

Segregate personal areas using physical boundaries as required by the personalities and ages of your children. Consider using folding screens or low bookcases placed back-to-back. You may even choose to build real walls to separate the living areas. Bunk beds are another good solution for young children because they provide some bedtime privacy.

Each child will bring her own style to the room. The main goal should not be to coordinate everything; opt for neutral wall colors and furnishings, and then let each child decorate her portion of the room with her personal style. Bedding, wall art, and other details will give each youngster a sense of ownership of the space. If you want the room to have a more unified look, try incorporating an agreed-upon design, such as a particular color palette or theme. Then each occupant can design her space within the theme perimeters.

LEFT: Bunk beds maximize the space in this shared bedroom festooned with pennants from the two kids' favorite sports teams.

adapting as the child grows

KIDS GROW UP FAST. Wallpaper that's perfect for a 3-year-old will likely need to be replaced as the child matures. The more age-specific the initial design of the room, the sooner the eventual redesign will come.

To make the process of "growing a room" go smoothly, consider keeping big purchases, such as carpeting and large light fixtures, and overall jobs, such as wallpaper and paint, relatively neutral in style. Select materials that will not only look great in your youngster's room, but also stand the test of time as the child enters the teen years. Instead of traditional pastel pink or baby blue walls, think about such shades as sunflower yellow, moss green, china blue, or other hues that work as well with bins of toys as they do with movie posters.

For items that can be picked up and moved around, such as rugs, lamps, and bookcases, pick simple styles that can be used in other parts of the home as they outlive their usefulness in this room. Something as simple as a coat of paint can change a piece from cartoon-style to classic.

ABOVE: Light walls and plaid window treatments will grow with this child. Baby-inspired accents, such as the wallpaper border and small chair, will be easy to remove to create a more mature decorating theme in the future.

FOR STYLE, JUST ADD ACCENTS

Give your child's room personality and vibrancy by adding details that are easy to alter as he grows older.

CLASSIC HARDWOOD FLOORING can be covered by a **rug** that's simple to replace later.

LAMPS can be added, taken away, or swapped out as the child's tastes and lighting needs change.

FURNITURE can be repainted as **color schemes** change, while accessories, such as **linens** and **artwork**, can be replaced with fresh versions.

Using these types of items to expand on a favorite hobby or theme makes it easy for you to evolve the room's decor right along with your child's developing interests.

bedroom storage

ONE OF THE BEST WEAPONS in the constant battle to persuade youngsters to clean up their rooms is to furnish a play space that offers plenty of easily accessible storage. That means drawers, cubbies, shelves, bins, jars, chests, boxes, and cabinets all should be within the child's reach.

BELOW: A former closet becomes an alcove perfectly sized for a changing table. It can be reverted easily when the child no longer needs diapering.

ABOVE: Storage can be worked into dormers and odd spaces with recessed drawers or shelves. LEFT: For the young girl who scores a television for her room, this space-saving corner armoire provides a convenient place for favorite games and movies.

STORAGE SHORTCUTS

GRAB SPACE WHERE YOU CAN. Unless your child has a trundle bed, the space under the bed provides useful storage for toys and games. Organize these items with stylish wheeled baskets or bins that roll under the bed. Or make your own by attaching casters to old dresser drawers.

RETHINK THE CLOSET. The standard-size bedroom closet yields loads of storage space for a child—but not with the single rod found in many closets. Instead, implement a system to convert the space into a practical array of cubbies and shelves. Complete the project yourself with plastic-coated wire shelving that's sold and cut to size at Lowe's, or consider hiring a contractor to build your system.

DIVIDE IT UP. Spacious shelves and bins will only lead to piles of odds and ends. After all, many toys contain dozens or even hundreds of parts. Mix sets of toy soldiers, plastic locking blocks, and miniature race cars in one toy bin, and you have a mess. Children need storage that has plenty of dividers and segments for sorting all of their belongings.

LEAVE IT OPEN. Young kids manage better with open shelves and cubbies where they can keep visual inventory of their toys than with storage inside drawers and behind doors.

FIND A PLACE FOR EVERYTHING. Spend some time organizing so that all of your child's treasures have proper places. Then stick to that organization whenever you clean the room and make sure that your child understands the system. You might even want to mark these locations using color-coded stickers, small drawings printed from computer clip art, or printed labels for kids who are able to read.

SUBTRACT WHEN YOU ADD. As your child collects more possessions, try to weed out the items he has outgrown. You could even ask him to help decide what needs to be discarded in order to make room for exciting new belongings. Old gear can be handed-down to friends or relatives or donated to charity.

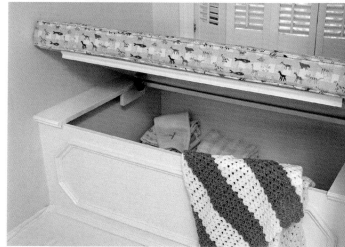

LEFT: A modular wire-shelving system from Lowe's is easy to adapt as he needs more space for clothing and less for toys. BELOW: Rustic baskets hold books and small knickknacks while maximizing the under-bed storage.

LEFT AND ABOVE: A window seat built into a small nook stores clothing or toys while creating a spot for story time. A safety hinge keeps little fingers from getting pinched. The clever combination of a roller shade and plantation shutters allows for easy light control.

storing clothing

A CLOSET WITH A SINGLE ROD hung at 65 to 68 inches does not work well for kids. And dressers are not particularly user-friendly either, at least until your child is tall enough to look into the upper drawers. Thankfully, there are many options that offer your youngster easy access to clothing and accessories.

THIS PAGE: Paint and organizational accessories from Lowe's transform this unfinished armoire into an infant's closet. Hooks, a closet rod, and a multilevel towel bar create space for clothing and linens.

CLOSET SYSTEMS If the room has a closet, install a system—a combination of shelves, cubbies, and drawers that help to maximize useful space. The best choice for young kids may be a modular system that can be rearranged as needs change.

ARMOIRES AND WARDROBES If a closet isn't available, use a freestanding piece of furniture. Look for a unit that has plenty of interior cubbies and shelves as well as low-lying drawers that are easily accessible for your child.

BUILT-IN CUBBIES Another option is to hire a contractor to build shelving along a wall. That way, clothes storage is part of the built-in cabinetry that also provides room for books and toys, display space, and even a window seat or a desk that

ABOVE: Wire drawers, shelves, and baskets make it easy to put away toys. Everyday items are placed within a child's reach, while less frequently needed items are stored higher to utilize the closet's vertical space.

THIS PAGE: The multiple components in this closet system for a young man add up to easy organization and maintenance. They tackle a variety of storage needs when fashioned with shelves, drawers, and baskets. Accessories stay neat in hanging organizers.

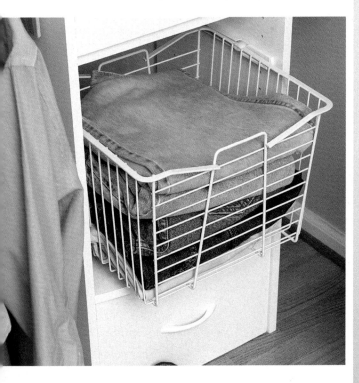

pulls out. If your child is old enough to dress himself, make sure that you store clothing within his reach. Doors and drawers provide storage that can be closed off to hide clutter. But if you are willing to embrace the colorful charm of clothing storage out in the open, use exposed cubbies. When a child is able to see his clothes—without having to pull out a drawer or open a door—he is much more likely to pick out his own outfit and dress himself.

HOOKS AND PEGS Several low hooks on the back of a closet door, a wall-mounted coatrack, or some Shaker-style pegs on the side of a bunk bed make it quick and easy for little ones to hang up their pajamas, towels, hats, and jackets.

DIRTY-CLOTHES FUN Persuading your child to use a hamper isn't always easy. One good trick is to make a sport of putting away dirty laundry using a basketball-hoop hamper, which is similar to a regular indoor hoop that hangs from a door, except that the net is actually a large hamper bag.

ABOVE: Double rods in a nursery closet accommodate tiny clothes while also leaving room for future growth. BELOW: Two rods, multiple shelves, and other storage items keep belongings for a young lady neat and tidy.

collectibles and displays

MANY CHILDREN BEGIN COLLECTING treasures at a young age. They may accumulate seashells, baseball hats, autographs, dolls, model airplanes, or even rocks. And understandably, they want to display these items so that they can be admired and shown to family and friends. Most kids also like to show off their latest craft projects, stuffed animals, or other prized possessions. So their rooms need to include plenty of display surfaces to accommodate orderly presentations.

Provide ample shelving within your child's reach—which means at or below eye level. You can accomplish this with freestanding furniture, shelves that hang from wall-mounted tracks, or even built-in cabinetry. But no matter which method you choose, it's essential that the shelves are sturdy, safe, and adjustable, so they can be rearranged as your child grows. (See the Safety Checklist on page 11 for tips on how to install bookshelves and tall furniture properly.)

TOP, RIGHT: A decorative screen is perfect for photos and keepsakes.
MIDDLE, RIGHT: Increase display space by attaching rolled corkboard to any wall—you can even paint the corkboard to match the wall color.
BOTTOM, RIGHT: Rope moulding dresses up a simple shelf that stores educational items and favorite treasures above a desk.

DISPLAY TIPS

• Cover an entire wall with corkboard, and you've fashioned a bulletin board where your child can hang her latest art projects (as long as she is old enough to use thumbtacks).

• Create an arts-and-crafts shelf for the youngster's latest masterpieces, including school projects and home hobbies.

• Buy standard-size picture frames at an art-supply store, and use them to create a gallery of your child's work. Replace with new pieces every six months.

• Hang objects on the wall with shadow boxes, which are deep frames used for displaying three-dimensional objects. Some boxes have room for only one item, while others provide many individual cubbies for displaying numerous keepsakes.

• Craft a decorative folding screen from wood, and cover it with corkboard, dry-erase board, or chalkboard paint. Your child can use it to display artwork or write messages.

LEFT: Clothespins and spray paint transform this wooden garden trellis into a snapshot gallery.

Here's a unique use for something usually found in the kitchen. This plate rack is filled with books and toys.

room for play, study, and hobbies

EVEN WITH THE MYRIAD OF furniture and gear that's needed to provide comfortable sleeping arrangements plus storage for childhood must-haves, the bedroom also should offer open spaces where the child can play, work, and create. Such areas can, of course, be located in playrooms or elsewhere in the house, but if space allows, be sure to include activity zones in your child's bedroom as well.

DESKS A child's table is a great work surface for all sorts of projects. But by the time your little one enters grade school, he should have his own desk for completing homework. Having a dedicated well-lit work area helps to teach children good study habits. And be certain that the desk is located far enough away from any distractions such as televisions and video games.

PLAY AREA Set aside some floor space where your child can play with friends or spread out with his favorite toys and books. A soft, flat surface is ideal, so consider rubber tiles or a carpet with a

ABOVE: This magnetic "doorman" can keep little ones busy for hours. Cut metal sheets into desired shapes. Spray the pieces with metal primer, and then use spray paint in colors of your choice. Attach the sheets to the door with ½-inch metal screws. Add a child-size table to provide more space for play.

COMPUTER WORKSTATIONS FOR KIDS

Whether you set up a separate computer area just for your kids or allot them time on the family computer, they need a comfortable, efficient work environment. Otherwise, they can learn bad habits that could lead to difficulties as adults. Here are some guidelines from the Cornell University Ergonomics Research Group.

• **ADJUST THE CHAIR AND COMPUTER SCREEN** so that your child's head is not tilted up or down. His feet should be flat on the ground with knees bent at about 90 degrees from the upper leg; use a foot rest, such as a stool, if necessary. And the chair should support his back. Put a pillow behind him if extra padding is necessary.

• **USE AN ADJUSTABLE KEYBOARD TRAY** to position the mouse and keyboard so that your child's elbows are bent at 90 degrees with his wrists fairly straight.

• **ADJUST THE TASK LIGHTING** to ensure that your child is not experiencing glare from the screen.

• **MANAGE COMPUTER TIME** so that your child doesn't spend more than 30 minutes at the computer before taking a break to walk around and stretch. Set a stopwatch, a kitchen timer, or the clock on the computer to alert the youngster that it's time for a break.

• **ALSO, IF YOUR CHILD IS LEFT-HANDED,** arrange a one-button mouse on the left side of the keyboard when he's computing.

LEFT: Study space for two is a snap with these coordinating furniture pieces. Each child has a desk as well as shelving and drawer space.

ABOVE: For the older child, a built-in bench and plenty of cushions turn this window nook into a spot for reading.

tight weave. (For more information, turn to the "Flooring" section of this chapter on page 42.) The area should be surrounded by low storage shelves that your youngster can reach, and it should be equipped with plenty of adjustable task lighting. Make the space flexible with portable furnishings, such as beanbag chairs and a table that rides on casters, that are easy to move out of the way.

CRAFTS CORNER Turn any underutilized area into an arts-and-crafts station where messes are welcome. Cover the floor with a loose piece of vinyl or linoleum (secure with heavy tape or weigh it down with furniture, if needed), and line the walls with washable wallpaper or paint. Provide an easel or table and a cubby filled with a variety of craft supplies, such as paint, glue, and construction paper. Hang art smocks on a hook, and keep an array of supplies nearby for cleaning up messes, preferably behind locked childproof doors for safety.

<<< CREATIVE PLAY

This art station was created with a parts bin mounted to the wall above a drapery rod cut to fit a roll of builder's paper. A simple work surface nearby keeps crafting contained to one part of the room.

<<< EASY REACH

A garden apron attached to the edge of this table provides instant storage for art supplies.

walls

THE WALLS OFFER a primary source of character for any room, so take advantage of the numerous color and design options. If you're artistic, consider covering one wall of your kindergartner's room with a mural of undersea creatures or a baseball game. Or, you might paint zebra stripes on the nursery ceiling to pique your newborn's visual interest. But if you want your paint job to endure, choose a simple scheme that's not age-specific (and let the room's accessories make a statement).

When choosing wall color, think about the mood you want to create. Reds, yellows, and oranges are considered warm hues because they grab our attention and energize us. For a bedroom, you might prefer cool tones, such as blues, greens, and violets, which are reminiscent of nature and have a calming effect. Regardless of the specific color, avoid soft pastel or bold pure versions. Instead, choose a shade that contains some black or brown—these are generally more sophisticated, so your child may not outgrow the wall color as quickly. Although flat and eggshell sheens are common, glossier finishes such as satin, pearl, or semigloss are easier to wipe clean.

Wallpaper is another option to enliven the room, and there are many fun designs, including storybook characters, animals, geometric shapes, and even full-scale murals. Use vinyl wallpaper, which is washable and easier to remove in the future. And again, try to choose a design you and your child will be happy with for at least a couple of years. Otherwise, you might prefer prepasted borders, murals, and wallpaper cutouts that stick on the wall and will peel off easily later.

TOP, RIGHT: Create bedtime scenery by wallpapering the nursery ceiling. Here, it continues down a portion of the wall. A chair rail with decorative knobs finishes the line between wallpaper and paint. RIGHT: Lime green paint sets off crisp white wainscot, which includes inset pieces of magnetic whiteboard.

READY-MADE DECOR

Coordinating ensembles of decorative items make it easy to dress up your child's walls. You'll find a variety to choose from at Lowe's, and most will include the following items.

- wallpaper borders
- paint stamps
- night-lights
- switch plates
- three-dimensional wall art

ABOVE: Vertical stripes in shades of lavender dress up this room for an older child. For an interesting contrast, crown moulding was installed a few inches lower than the ceiling to provide a starting point for the sage green color on the ceiling.

safety
checklist

LEAD PAINT

Test kits can be purchased to check your paint for the presence of lead, but it's safe to assume that any house built before 1978 (when lead paint was banned) contains some lead paint. Lead paint chips and the dust created from sanding can be harmful to the adult who's sanding, as well as others in the house. Be sure to follow these simple safety precautions when dealing with lead in your home.

• **NEVER SAND LEAD PAINT** because it creates microscopic particles that can be inhaled. Scrape lead paint only after you've cleared out the room and sealed it by securing plastic sheeting over doors with tape. After scraping the paint, you will need to clean all room surfaces thoroughly using a HEPA filtration vacuum and soap and water.

• **PEELING PAINT** should be scraped away first. Then the surface should be sealed with a lead sealant, which is basically a thick paint designed to hold loose chips in place. This product generally contains a bitter flavoring just in case a baby happens to put a peeling chip in her mouth.

• **WHEN YOU PERFORM** your seasonal housecleaning, be sure to wipe down windowsills and baseboards with a detergent that contains at least 5 percent phosphorous.

• **FOR MORE INFORMATION** on the proper ways to deal with lead paint, you may contact the National Lead Information Center at epa.gov/lead/nlic.htm or 1-800-424-5323. A downloadable pamphlet is available from the U.S. Department of Housing and Urban Development at hud.gov/offices/lead/helpyourself/Lead.pdf.

HOW TO: stripe it

Clever paint treatments are easier than you think. For the look shown on page 6, follow these steps.

STEP 1: Coat the walls with latex primer. (Note: If the existing paint is oil based, use an oil-based primer.) Measure and mark the guidelines around the room for the 1.41-inch white stripes. (See illustration below.) Using a 4-inch roller, paint white bands (American Tradition, Snow Cap #7003-8, satin) around the room per the guidelines. Rough edges will be covered.

STEP 2: Measure and mark 20 inches below the bottom edge of the crown moulding for the first stripe. (Note: You may need to adjust measurements to fit the height of your space.) From this first line, measure 21⅜ inches down, and make another mark for the second stripe. Repeat at 21⅜ inches below the second mark. Using a level, lightly draw a straight pencil line around the room at each mark to position the tape. (Tip: Use a pencil in a color close to that of the paint so guidelines will fade away visually.)

STEP 3: Affix painter's tape below each guideline marked in Step 2. Firmly press tape down to keep paint from bleeding underneath.

STEP 4: Paint stripes in alternating colors (American Tradition, Spring Lawn #6006-9C, satin, and American Tradition, Star Gazer #4008-8B, satin).

STEP 5: Gently remove the tape to reveal sharp white bands. (Tip: Let the paint dry overnight before you remove tape from the walls.)

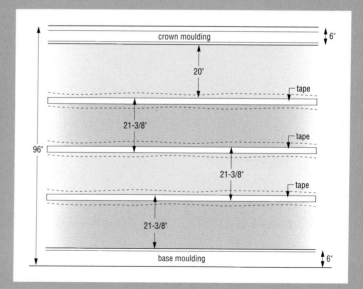

color cues

You can transform a room when you change the color.

CONSIDER THESE TIPS.
• Light hues make rooms look larger. Conversely, dark shades make them seem cozy.

• A semigloss or gloss finish intensifies a color, while a flat or eggshell finish subdues it.

• Brighten a room that has no windows, or one that has small windows, using a sunny, light-filled hue.

Shop Smart:

SIGNATURE COLORS

The American Tradition Signature Colors collection at Lowe's includes a variety of colors and personalities that are as beautiful as they are durable and scrubbable. Exclusive to Lowe's, Signature Colors achieve one-coat coverage through a paint technology called Duramax Ti3. An infusion of titanium in the paint formula provides superior color definition in a wide spectrum. In addition, high-quality 100% acrylic resins are added, resulting in a long-lasting finish. This means your walls will withstand washings and remain as bright as when they were first painted.

For more information on American Tradition Signature Colors, log on to Lowes.com/Signature. In addition to the huge variety of regular American Tradition shades, Signature Colors are available in color families such as Laura Ashley Home, Eddie Bauer Home, Waverly Home Classics, and more.

KIDS SPEND A LOT OF TIME on the floor—reading, playing, and roughhousing. So the floor itself needs to be as comfortable as it is durable. If the bedroom has wood floors or clean, thick wall-to-wall carpeting, you already have a good surface. If you need to replace your flooring, here are some of the best options.

WALL-TO-WALL CARPETING With a thick pad underneath, this is the most comfy surface for a child's bedroom, plus it helps keep the room warm and block noise coming from other parts of the house. Look for a nylon carpet to avoid potential allergic reactions to natural wool, but if allergies or asthma are a concern consider avoiding carpeting. A room air filter or central air-conditioning with a HEPA air filter will help remove irritants from the air.

AREA RUG A bound area rug provides the same comfort as wall-to-wall carpeting, plus it can be sent out for cleaning. It also allows you to leave a section of floor bare for blocks, train sets, and other toys that need a stable base.

Shop Smart: CHOOSING CARPET

twist pile

shag pile

loop pile

velvet pile

Carpet is a vital style decision, but its livability is the key. For example, short-napped wool carpet holds up to traffic and is also a safe choice for most who will be using the room, whether their steps are steady or they require assistance. Also consider the following general tips as you narrow down your search.

CARPET TYPES
Woven carpets tend to be more costly because of their weave, while the tufted and bonded varieties are the least expensive. Most household carpet is the tufted kind, which means that the yarn is stitched on a pre-woven backing.

The pile of the four main types of tufted carpets—twist pile, shag pile, loop pile, and velvet pile—is cut to different heights and forms unique designs.

CARPET GRADES
Carpet is graded according to durability. Some types are suited for high-traffic areas, others for light wear. Higher quality carpet, which typically has a jute backing, requires a separate underlay. This type should be installed professionally. (Note: Lowe's can provide guaranteed professional installation.) Less expensive carpets have a foam backing and don't require an underlay.

ABOVE: Soft, low-pile carpeting gives this child room for play. ABOVE, RIGHT: Hardwood, an easy-to-maintain flooring choice, can be softened with a fun rug. Many carpet styles can be ordered in pieces that you can have bound to create an area rug.

Use a thick pad as you would under wall-to-wall carpeting. Or, you can have a piece of actual wall-to-wall carpeting bound to the appropriate size for the room.

RUBBER TILES These squares of brightly colored foam rubber interlock like puzzle pieces and combine the plushness of carpet with the flatness of wood floors. They are easy to install yourself. And when you are ready for something new, they're easy to remove because they are not glued down. As an inexpensive option, they make a particularly good choice for play areas.

safety ✓checklist

WINDOWS AND DOORS

Prevent injuries by installing a few safety gadgets on your windows and doors. You can add key locks to your windows, making them harder for a child to open from the inside or for a burglar to open from the outside.

Be aware of miniblinds and other window treatments with unsafe pull cords that could strangle a child who becomes tangled in them. You can purchase small attachments at Lowe's that will keep the cords wound up. Or, if you prefer, newer window treatments are available that are cordless or have two or more individual control cords (rather than those that loop or attach to one another).

LEFT: Control access to off-limit rooms by covering doorknobs with special plastic covers that keep little hands from turning the knobs.

furniture

YOU CAN BUY JUNIOR-SIZE BEDS that mimic everything from Noah's ark to a race car to a fancy four-poster. Many have rails to prevent the child from falling out and a low profile to make it easy to hop aboard. Still, you may prefer to buy your child an adult-size twin or full bed as soon as she outgrows the crib. These larger beds will last for decades, and there are plenty of other opportunities to incorporate fun decorative details in the bedroom.

You'll face a similar decision between child- and adult-size furnishings when you select shelving and other storage cabinetry. You may decide to buy a brightly colored child-size unit and replace or repaint it later, or you can select a simple adult-size piece and let your child grow into it.

For other bedroom furniture, however, it is essential that you purchase pieces sized for kids. Little people require little tables, chairs, cubbies, and desks. If the furniture is too big or too small, it will be more difficult for your child to adopt good posture and sitting habits. The average 3-year-old needs a table that's 15 inches off the floor and a chair with an 8-inch-high seat. By the time she turns 7, she needs a 19-inch table and an 11-inch-high seat. And by age 12, she will have grown into a 23-inch table and a 13-inch-high seat.

Bedroom sets are available in all sizes with matching colors and details for kids of all ages. Or, a less expensive way to achieve the same look is to buy unfinished furniture: sturdy, solid-wood pieces that you paint yourself. These usually are available in a wide range of sizes and configurations. Paint with a bright, fun color scheme to create a matching set. You can add and subtract pieces—and repaint them in more mature colors—as your little one grows up, and you'll always have bedroom furniture that is appropriate for your child's age.

Another good solution for meeting your youngster's ever-changing needs is to select adjustable or modular furniture. Chairs and desks that adjust can be set at different heights to accommodate growth spurts. Modular furniture is made up of individual

ABOVE: A simple chest of drawers can be accessorized to complement any motif, and a bedside chair offers a cozy spot for a bedtime story. LEFT AND BELOW: Simple unfinished furniture can be dressed up with paint and playful hardware. Both the color and the pulls can be changed in accordance with the child's interests.

components, including desks, shelves, drawers, cabinets, and tables, which can be arranged in different configurations to meet your requirements. You also can add new components to the room in the future.

Beanbag chairs make terrific seating solutions for kids' rooms. They have no hard edges that can pose a hazard to little heads, they conform to your child's body size, and they are easy for children to maneuver around the space as needed.

clever lighting

IF YOU ARE BUILDING A NEW HOUSE OR DOING A REMODELING PROJECT, you can wire in a host of different fixtures to provide ambient light as well as task lighting for such activities as reading in bed, playing, and working at a desk or table. But if you live in an older home, your child's room probably has only one fixture in the middle of the ceiling. You could hire an electrician to wire in track lighting over the desk and sconces by the bed. Or make the most of what you have already, and consider these tips.

• **Upgrade the ceiling fixture.** Many fixtures are rated for only 60-watt bulbs, which don't emit much light. It's unsafe to use a brighter bulb in a low-wattage fixture (if the fixture does not have a maximum wattage label, assume it's limited to 60 watts). But you can replace the fixture with one that takes multiple bulbs or is rated for a higher wattage bulb.

• **Add a dimmer switch.** Replace the on-off switch with a dimmer, and you'll be able to control just how much light the ceiling fixture gives off. Set the level very low and it can become a night-light or allow you just enough illumination to check on a sleeping child.

• **Install plug-in options.** Corded fixtures offer additional lighting, and a sconce or swing-arm lamp can provide good task lighting for bedside reading. But avoid halogen bulbs in rooms frequented by children, because those bulbs can get dangerously hot. Install the fixture firmly, and fasten the cord securely.

headboard project

HOW TO: paint it

Eye-catching headboards are the focal point in this bedroom. The simple design reverses the usual arched shape of many headboards with a dip like the scoop neck of a T-shirt. Even a beginner can achieve this attractive plaid finish—the only skill required is patience.

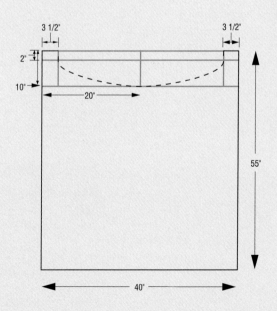

STEP 1: Draw the guidelines and the curve onto the plywood according to the illustration at left. Cut out the headboard with a jigsaw.

STEP 2: Smooth all edges using a random orbit sander.

STEP 3: Prime the board, including the edges, and allow to dry.

STEP 4: Apply two or three coats of khaki-colored paint to the board, being sure to cover the edges. Allow paint to dry thoroughly after each coat.

STEP 5: Find the center of the board, and mark it with a pencil. Measure and mark 1 inch to the left and right of the center. Using a T-square, draw vertical lines down the length of the board at each of these points.

STEP 6: From the left vertical line, work left to the edge of the board by measuring and marking every 2 inches.

Repeat the measuring and marking process on the right side of the board.

STEP 7: The center 2 inches will be painted the solid red color, so begin taping to the outside of the first two vertical lines that you drew on the board. Next, tape off the remaining areas that are to be painted red by taping off every other 2-inch space.

STEP 8: Paint two or three coats of red paint to create the vertical lines of the plaid design. Once the paint is dry, carefully peel off the tape.

STEP 9: Just as you measured and marked every 2 inches vertically in Steps 5 and 6, repeat the same process horizontally for the lighter red stripe. Measure 2 inches down from the top (starting on the "bedposts"), to begin. Tape as in Step 7.

STEP 10: Create a lighter red glaze by mixing one part of red paint with one part of clear glaze. (Tip: A little glaze goes a long way, so you don't have to use the entire can of glaze.)

STEP 11: Using a foam brush, apply one coat of the red glaze to create the horizontal stripes of the plaid. Repeat this process until all of the horizontal stripes are glazed.

STEP 12: While the glaze is still tacky, carefully remove the tape. Touch up the stripes as necessary to ensure clean, straight edges.

STEP 13: When dry, apply two coats of clear Polycrylic to protect the finish.

STEP 14: Attach to the bed frame. Drill two ¼-inch holes on each bottom side of the headboard. (The exact placement of these holes will depend on individual bed frames.) Use carriage bolts, flat washers, and hex nuts to fasten the headboard to the bed frame through the drilled holes and the appropriate openings in the frames.

Lowe's Shopping List
(for one twin bed)

Materials
- 1 (¾-inch-thick) 4- x 8-foot sheet of plywood
- primer
- khaki paint (American Tradition, Milestone #6007-1B, satin)
- red paint (American Tradition, Radiant Red #1009-3, satin)
- (2-inch) painter's tape
- clear glaze (Valspar Decorative Effects)
- Polycrylic
- 2 (¼-inch) #20 x 1-inch carriage bolts
- 2 (¼-inch) hex nuts
- 2 (¼-inch) flat washers

Tools
- scissors
- pencil
- jigsaw
- random orbit sander
- tape measure
- medium-grit sandpaper disc
- (4-inch) paintbrush
- T-square
- (2-inch) foam paintbrush
- drill and bits

Skill level: Beginner
Rough cost estimate: $150*
Rough time estimate: 2 days
*Does not include applicable taxes, which vary by market.

accessories

IT'S IN THE DETAILS of your child's room that you will infuse creativity and personality with the most ease. And there is no need for you to hold yourself back because it's simple to replace these accessories when your child loses interest or outgrows them.

DECORATING SETS The most effortless way to accessorize your child's room is with a collection of specialty decor items. Choose from the dozens of design themes available for all ages and genders, and then purchase the paint, wallpaper, lamps, bookends, wall hooks, shelves, and more in that same motif. Expectant parents find this decorating method particularly convenient because it is easy to register for the entire collection prior to baby showers.

MIX-AND-MATCH You also can combine individual accessories to create your own personal theme. Pick a motif, a color, or something unique to tie the design together. For example, your concept could be centered around vibrant geometric shapes; thus, all the accessories you make or buy would be composed of shapes such as circles, squares, or triangles in different primary colors. Mixing-and-matching also makes it easy to incorporate family heirlooms or toys in your child's room.

CRAFTY CREATIONS If you're artistic, you may decide to freehand your own designs on accessories in the room. Popular choices include jungle animals, sports gear, and even favorite foods. Or purchase stencils in your chosen theme and use them to create your decorations.

RIGHT: The playful design of the bed is complemented by pretty linens and accessories.

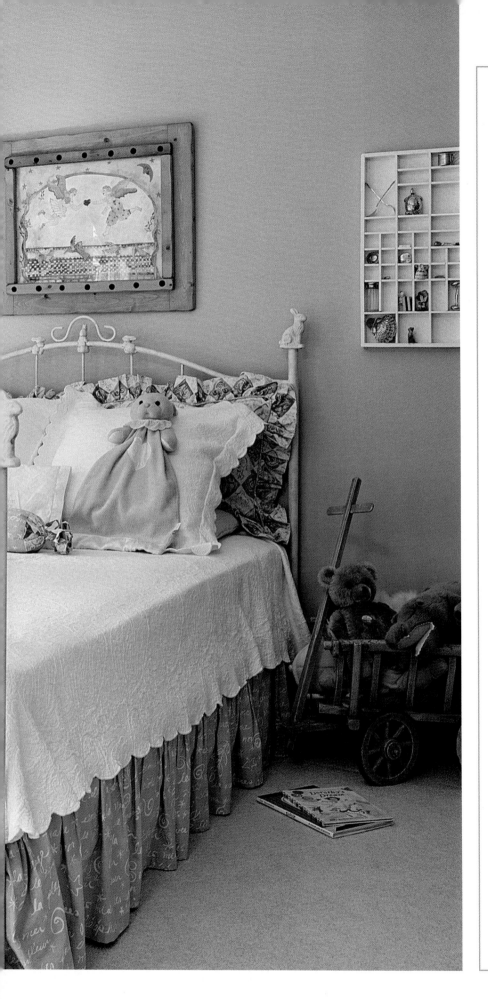

CARD ART

Create attractive art from greeting cards. Cut three (10-inch-long) pieces from a 3-foot-long poplar 1 x 8. Prime, and let dry. Center a card on each board, and mark the edges to denote a border. (Tip: Our 5- x 7-inch cards worked well with the 8- x 10-inch boards. Adjust the size of the board accordingly to fit cards of varying dimensions.) Remove the card, and paint a striped border in cream (American Tradition, Pontoon White #7006-13, semigloss) and green (American Tradition, Parisian Mist #7005-6, semigloss). When dry, affix the card to the board with spray adhesive. Drill two holes (see the photo below for placement) along the top of each board. Insert a screw eye into each hole; attach a 10-inch piece of ribbon by knotting it on the screw eyes. Use ribbon to hang your artwork.

BIG LOOK

Lowe's Shopping List

Materials

- 1 (¼-inch-thick) 4- x 8-foot sheet of plywood
- primer
- base coat (American Tradition, Lazy Sun #3006-6A, semigloss)
- second coat for carrot (American Tradition, Woodlawn Marmalade #2003-6B, semigloss)
- third coat for carrot (American Tradition, La Fonda Spanish Dancer #2005-3B, semigloss)
- accents for carrot (American Tradition, La Fonda Antique Red #2002-5A, semigloss)
- second coat for leaves (American Tradition, Crocodile Smile #6005-7C, semigloss)
- third coat for leaves (American Tradition, Lucky Clover #6005-8B, semigloss)
- numbers (American Tradition, Dark Kettle Black #4011-2, semigloss)

Tools

- spiral saw
- tape measure
- (1½-inch) paintbrush
- utility brush set
- medium sanding sponge
- safety glasses
- (½-inch) brass nails

Skill level: Beginner/intermediate

Rough cost estimate: $190

Rough time estimate: 1 day (including drying time)

For a template of this carrot, log on to LowesCreativeIdeas.com, click on Archive, and click on "A Child's Growth Chart" under Family Projects.

A CHILD'S GROWTH CHART

Start keeping a record of precious childhood milestones with this garden-style growth chart. Use a pen to mark your child's height, and label the month and year next to it. This provides a fantastic way to watch your little one grow, plus it becomes a delightful memory maker.

STEP 1: Sketch a freehand carrot-like shape onto the plywood. (See "Lowe's Shopping List" above to find out how to locate a carrot template on the Lowe's Web site.) The design should be about 40 inches wide and 72 inches high.

STEP 2: Following the directions included with your spiral saw, cut out your carrot shape from the plywood. Sand all rough edges smooth.

STEP 3: Prime the entire board, and allow to dry.

STEP 4: Layer paint colors according to the photograph above or your own design. Allow drying time between different coats.

STEP 5: Run a tape measure vertically along the chart, and mark feet and inches lightly on the board with a pencil. (Note: Consider whether or not you need to account for any base moulding. For example, if there is a 4-inch base moulding in the room, you'll need to factor in this measurement on your chart.) Use black paint to cover the foot and inch pencil markings. Finally, clarify the dimensions by painting the correct number at each foot increment.

STEP 6: Secure the chart to the wall with brass nails.

LEFT: This dressing table commands even more attention when placed underneath an elegant mirror surrounded by a collection of hats.

ABOVE: Hand-painted stripes on the wall, along with lively accessories, give this nursery an animated style.

ART OPTIONS To keep artwork inexpensive and interchangeable, consider framing things such as movie posters, greeting cards, vintage fabrics, or interesting wrapping papers. When framed, almost anything can pass for artwork. Your child's own paintings or other creations also make nice additions to the decor. And to avoid the constant patching of nail holes, create a gallery of shelves from Lowe's so that the artwork can be swapped out or moved around. A variety of sizes and styles are available.

FAMILY PHOTOS Use a collage frame to hang pictures of family. It's an excellent way to teach a youngster about his relatives.

CEILING ART Since kids spend so much time lying down—both in bed and on the floor—the ceiling provides a wonderful decorating opportunity. A classic approach is to paint it to look like a blue sky with a few puffy clouds overhead. Another option is to use glow-in-the-dark planet and star stickers to create a nighttime planetarium. You may want to think three-dimensionally and hang various coordinating objects from the ceiling. If you are good with a sewing machine, make pillows with vibrant fabrics in the shapes of birds, clouds, stars, airplanes, or whatever might interest your child, and then hang them at varying heights around the room.

kids'
bathroo

This dream bath features
two sinks, ample shelves
and drawers for personal
items, and a separate space
for the toilet and bathtub.

ms t

TO A CHILD, THE BATHROOM can be one of the most enjoyable rooms in the house, and it also can be one of the most challenging. Hours of happy splashing and swimming—once you get her in the tub, that is—take place here. But this is also the room where she learns important (and often difficult) lessons about everything from brushing her teeth to using the potty. A child's bathroom should offer a fun atmosphere, where she feels comfortable, safe, and confident, while providing a space that's conducive to learning those lessons.

Whether you are gearing up for a major bathroom remodel, a minor renovation, or a weekend decorating project, it is not always practical to install somewhat permanent fixtures that are sized for kids or detailed with youthful designs. These would be outgrown in a few years and could turn off potential buyers when it's time to sell the house. Stick with standard-size fixtures in classic colors and finishes. For example, brushed metal is a timeless, durable style. For walls and flooring, select colors that are relatively ageless—hues such as sand, caramel, peach, or sage are excellent choices. A stroll down the aisles at Lowe's will reveal numerous options in these long-lasting styles.

The real character of a child's bathroom should be attained through accessories: Colorful plastic boats, rubber ducks, and other tub toys are essentials for young children, of course. If the bathroom also must serve teenagers or adults, choose cheerful hues for everything from the wall paint to the shower curtain to the bath towels. A dramatic splash of color will lend the space a youthful look while ensuring that the rest of the family members feel at ease in the room.

simple renovations

A FEW MINOR IMPROVEMENTS can make a big difference in a bathroom's overall appearance and functionality. Upgrade this part of your home and make it more kid-friendly with simple strategies made possible by the tools and products you'll find at Lowe's.

FLOORING From energetic youngsters to busy teenagers, the bathroom floor is going to get wet. That's why tile is a popular choice for this room of the house. If yours already has a tile floor in good condition, you may need to simply caulk the seams or replace the existing caulk where the floor meets the bathtub and walls. Wood also is a surprisingly durable choice for bathrooms, and new laminate technology provides a considerable barrier against moisture and scratches. In fact, laminate is most likely your best bet for longevity in the bathroom's moist environment.

ABOVE: This ceramic tile, which has a skid-proof finish, makes a safe and durable flooring choice for a child's bathroom. The dark grout hides dirt well. RIGHT: Tile in most any style or material provides a great moisture-resistant surround for tubs and showers. It also can be arranged in a wide variety of patterns, offering stylish versatility.

safety ✓checklist

HOT WATER SAFETY

Any bathtub or shower used by children should have anti-scald protection. This device prevents bathers from getting burned when a toilet is flushed or cold water is turned on somewhere else in the house. If you're adding a bathroom or remodeling one, plumbing codes require a temperature-balance valve that eliminates scalding. In an existing bathroom, however, the temperature of your bath and shower water may be controlled by separate knobs for hot and cold. You'll need to add an anti-scald device if this is the case. A plumber can retrofit a single-lever pressure-balanced valve into your existing bathroom. The old knob holes—and the access hole the plumber may cut between them—will need to be tiled or covered with a decorative metal plate designed for this purpose.

A more straightforward solution is to install a shut-off valve that automatically stops the water flow if it reaches 114 degrees. A reset button allows water to be restarted at a lower temperature. Install this fitting on a shower pipe, or you may opt to purchase faucets, showerheads, and tub spouts that have a built-in automatic shut-off.

IMPROVE YOUR VENT FAN

Excess humidity in the bathroom can lead to mold and mildew growth on the walls and, in time, structural damage. So, it's crucial to have a bathroom vent fan and to make sure that it's used during any bath or shower. The fan should run for 20 minutes after all showers. The following simple solutions may help persuade children to comply with these rules.

- **CONNECT THE FAN TO THE CIRCUIT** for the overhead light so that anytime the light is on, the fan is on.

- **INSTALL A FAN WITH A BUILT-IN HUMIDISTAT** that automatically turns itself on and off based upon the amount of moisture in the air.

- **INVEST IN A WHISPER-QUIET VENT FAN.** Practically silent, these are more pleasant to operate.

WALLS The alcove around the tub should be surfaced with either tile or a fiberglass-reinforced plastic, such as acrylic or gel coat. Consider tile for the remainder of the walls, as well—at least as a 4- to 5-foot-tall wainscot. Alternatively, you can install a wooden wainscot, which is better than leaving the plaster or gypsum drywall exposed to splashing, but this option doesn't provide as much waterproofing as tile does. If you prefer wood, use beaded-board paneling, which is made from plywood or medium-density fiberboard. It is more resistant than solid wood to warping from humidity. Still, all surfaces of the wainscot—including the back and cut edges—should be primed and painted to help lock out moisture.

LIGHTING Ideally, a bathroom should feature an overhead light as well as sconces or vanity lights to illuminate the work areas—such as where your child brushes his teeth and washes his hands and face. In a shared bathroom, the same space Dad uses for shaving may double as a hair and makeup styling station for Mom and the girls. A light over the shower also is helpful. If your bathroom doesn't provide enough lighting, hire an electrician to wire for new fixtures. Keep in mind that plug-in lamps pose a hazard in bathrooms.

SINK FAUCET Unlike replacing a sink, installing a faucet is a simple job. Most importantly, it should be easy for any child to use. The single-handle faucet is a good choice for kids. If your sink has three faucet holes with the outermost placed 4 inches apart, install a single-handle faucet that has a plate to cover the two extra holes. If the sink's holes are farther than 4 inches apart, a single-handle unit is not an option without replacing the sink. In that case, look for a double-handle faucet with controls that rotate effortlessly.

LEFT: Adding or replacing lights in a bathroom is an easy way to improve style and functionality.

Recessed lights provide general illumination for this bathroom, while elegant sconces give the vanity area extra task lighting.

shared spaces

IN A PERFECT WORLD, every home would feature a master bathroom, a guest bathroom, a children's bathroom, and an additional bathroom for the main living space. In the real world, many households have a shortage of "facilities." Sometimes parents share one bathroom and the kids share another. In other households, family members all use the same one. Once youngsters reach an age where showering is part of their wake-up routine, the morning rush can become pretty hectic.

There are a number of ways to make bathrooms work well for everyone involved, whether or not your future plans include remodeling efforts.

IF YOU'RE REMODELING:

• Subdivide the space with walls, half walls, or translucent glass partitions to create private or semi-private areas for the toilet and bath. This way, more than one person can use the bathroom at the same time without compromising anyone's modesty.

• Install two sinks so that multiple family members can get ready simultaneously.

• Buy a substantial water heater, whether you share a bathroom or not, that can handle all of the family's baths and showers without leaving the last person out in the cold. For example, a two-person household might need a 40-gallon tank, while a five-person family with teenagers probably needs twice that capacity. A plumber can recommend the right tank size for your house. This decision is based upon a number of different factors, including the type of fuel used to heat your water.

• Install a high-volume bathroom vent fan to clear out the humidity that is created by multiple showers.

RIGHT AND FAR RIGHT: Dividing these baths into two distinct spaces helps morning routines move more efficiently and reduces disagreements over sink and shower time.

adding
a shower

One way to accommodate family members who bathe at the same time is to add a stand-alone shower, which takes up relatively little floor space. These units offer easier showering than combination tub-and-shower units do, because they don't require stepping in and out of a tub (a plus for kids who have just graduated to showers). One person can use the stand-alone while someone else washes up in the bathtub—or in the bathtub shower—to help relieve the morning rush.

ABOVE AND ABOVE, LEFT: Taking advantage of previously unused space, this attic bath maximizes the area with a long vanity that boasts drawers as well as a shelf. A shower and linen cabinet sit opposite.

WHETHER OR NOT YOU'RE REMODELING:

• Hang a large classroom-style clock on the bathroom wall to accommodate everyone's morning routines. Establish a bathroom schedule and hold everyone to it.

• Designate a particular shelf in the linen closet, a cabinet, or a drawer for each family member, where they can store their own bathroom supplies. (The smallest person should be given the lowest shelf, of course, and so on.)

• Provide an individual towel hook for each member of the household.

• Personalize everyone's washcloth and towel so that it's easy to keep track of whose is whose. You can do this by having them monogrammed or by assigning a different color to each person.

• Ask kids to get ready in their bedrooms, once they reach the age of primping in front of a mirror before school. A low table with a mirror and chair can make a terrific spot for the final preparations of the morning.

ABOVE: These drawers with dividers allow each child to organize her own area. RIGHT: When it comes to kids' bathrooms, easy-to-access storage is the key to a neat space. Open shelves and plenty of drawers keep this area clutter-free.

Trend Update:

THE JUNIOR SUITE

Just as master suites are popular ways to provide adults with a private spa, a new breed of bed-and-bath combinations—the kids' suite—is becoming a hot remodeling option. The idea is to provide children with a bathroom next to their bedrooms, sometimes accessible through a separate door. That means you can create a bathroom that caters just to them, which is especially nice when they're old enough to be independent and relish their personal space.

BELOW: Two sinks and ample storage go a long way toward keeping siblings happy. Each child has plenty of space for her own toiletries, and lots of elbow room to boot.

MAKING YOUR BATHROOM MORE USER-FRIENDLY will increase the comfort level for kids, as well as grandparents, family members with disabilities, and less mobile guests who may visit on occasion.

• Place towel bars and hooks within reach of the shower.
• Lower light switches to about 36 inches from the floor, where they're accessible to children and wheelchair-bound residents. Use easy-to-operate rocker switches that glow when the light is not in use.
• Use oversize C-shaped pulls on vanities and cabinets. They are easier to grasp.
• Choose a toilet that's easy to flush. A push-button model is easier to use than a lever style.

• Install grab bars alongside the toilet and shower, making su they're anchored solidly to the framing of the wall. The accessories add needed safety for everyone, regardless of age physical ability, and newer models offer stylish accents.
• To make a bathroom wheelchair accessible, use a high toi (add an offset flange to raise an existing toilet 3 inches). Choo a roll-in shower, which is a roomy shower without a sill. Insta wall-hung sinks and countertops without cabinets underneath make them approachable for an individual in a wheelcha Under-counter clearance typically is required to be 29 inch high and 17 inches deep.
• Visit Lowes.com for more suggestions. Type "Universal Design into the search engine for ideas on how to make every room your home accessible to individuals of all ability levels.

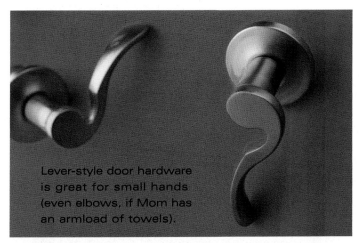

Lever-style door hardware is great for small hands (even elbows, if Mom has an armload of towels).

A thoughtfully placed robe hook keeps linens handy for the older children when they step out of the shower.

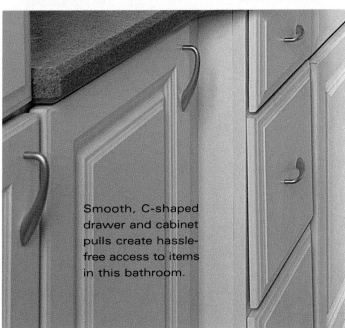

Smooth, C-shaped drawer and cabinet pulls create hassle-free access to items in this bathroom.

Bath and shower grab bars make bathing routines safer for all.

An open space beneath the wall-mounted sink makes it easier for small children to use while standing on a footstool or others to access while seated in a wheelchair.

storage

FROM TOWELS TO toothbrushes to tub toys, kids have a long list of bathroom supplies. But overflow linens and toiletries may be occupying any extra space in vanities and closets. Luckily, there are easy ways to add storage to any bathroom.

TOWEL HOOKS A child is much more likely to hang his towel on a hook than to fold it over a towel rod. So provide plenty of them at the appropriate height for young bathers. The most effective towel hooks feature two side-by-side prongs (each one is designed to hold a single towel).

TOY BINS AND BAGS As tough as it can be to compel a youngster to get in the tub, it's usually just as hard to get her out. Water play is fun, especially with plenty of ferry boats, tub crayons, and motorized fish with which to play. The best way to store this collection of bath toys is with a bin or bag that allows for water drainage and adheres to the tub wall with suction cups. Some of these handy containers even have trap doors for dumping the toys into the tub.

HANGING SHOWER CADDIES These simple, economical storage solutions keep adult bathing products and razors out of reach for children. A wire storage rack simply hooks over the shower pipe to provide overhead cargo space. Make sure that it hangs securely, without sliding down and over the showerhead, before loading it with heavy items.

CABINETRY Wall-hung cabinets do more than provide additional storage—they are also a decorative opportunity. You can find them in many sizes and configurations, but popular options are white cabinets with glass-paned or wooden doors and either chrome latches or wooden knobs. These are ideal for adult-only storage when mounted over the toilet or high on any open stretch of wall.

WALL-MOUNTED SHELVES A very current look is the glass shelf. Brackets

RIGHT: This small inset cabinet profits from the often-unused space behind shower fixtures, providing additional storage for linens and other bathroom necessities.
FAR RIGHT: A double towel bar holds extra towels for larger families and visitors.

MULTIPLE CHOICE

Although this bath is spacious, many of its storage options can be easily incorporated into smaller baths.

SPACE ABOVE the linen cabinet holds a container for extra linens or supplies.

A DOUBLE TOWEL BAR and towel ring keep linens organized and easy to find.

A TALL LINEN CABINET maximizes a narrow space, providing open and closed storage.

A ROBE HOOK placed conveniently next to the shower keeps bathrobes and towels close at hand.

HAVING A WEALTH OF DRAWERS AND CABINETS is a luxury in most bathrooms, but even a pair of cabinets can go a long way toward holding all of the toiletries and linens most families need.

WHAT A GREAT IDEA

BRINGING UP THE LAUNDRY

If your laundry area is located in the basement and you're remodeling a bathroom in the upstairs living quarters, consider relocating the laundry at the same time. Moving the washer and dryer closer to the majority of household bedrooms and bathrooms makes doing the wash far easier—and any family with kids cleans a lot of clothes. The machines can share the plumbing lines used for a bathroom; however, the dryer requires a high-voltage electrical line, and the washing machine should sit on a sturdy waterproof floor with a drain to handle overflows. And, of course, both require space. Stacking units can fit in an area the size of a small hallway closet.

fastened to the wall hold a narrow strip of thick tempered glass. Because they're glass, these shelves should be positioned out of reach for children. They're an ideal choice for installing alongside the sink—especially if it's a pedestal sink or one mounted on a small vanity that has limited counterspace around the basin.

HOTEL TOWEL RACKS Towel shelves made from chrome pipes are modeled after those often found in hotel bathrooms. Providing a wide shelf for folded towels and washcloths, these open-air units supply plentiful storage in a limited space. They mount on the wall of the bathtub alcove opposite the showerhead.

LINEN CABINETS A freestanding cabinet with interior shelves can serve as a makeshift linen closet. Look for a tall unit so that there is sufficient storage at a convenient height for adults, and anchor it to the wall with a childproofing tether strap. Then designate the lower levels as kids' storage, an ideal space for tucking away items such as bath toys and other child-appropriate items. Keep towels and other supplies in the upper compartments.

INSET SHELVING A great way to add shallow storage shelves virtually anywhere is to inset them into the wall. To do this, cut open the plaster or gypsum drywall and trim out the 14½-inch-wide, 3½-inch-deep space between the studs. This can be done on any interior wall where there aren't any electrical or plumbing lines.

HANGING DISPENSERS To keep the bathroom free of the clutter of bottles and tubes on the edge of a tub or sink, hang a dispenser on the shower wall or by the sink. At the push of a button, these convenient hand pumps dole out shampoo, conditioner, body wash, or lotion. Pumps are oftentimes more manageable for youngsters than the product's original container would have been, but they should be installed high enough to remain inaccessible for children who are not old enough to use them properly.

RIGHT: Shaker pegs along a chair rail keep linens at a comfortable height—high enough to remain off the floor but still low enough for little ones to reach. BELOW: Not only do these stylish shelves help maintain a neat and organized space, but they also prevent small items from getting lost behind larger objects.

ABOVE: Ample vanity storage is supplemented by inset shelving, ideal for keeping towels and other toiletries handy. RIGHT: A simple glass shelf keeps adult toiletries out of a toddler's reach. BELOW: This is a family-friendly bath. Wall cabinets store adult items, while lower drawers hold toys and children's supplies.

accessories

THE BEST WAY to ensure that a child feels at home in the bathroom is to accessorize with items that are fun, as well as helpful.

SHOWER CURTAINS All sorts of bright, colorful designs are available. For younger children, look for one with fun images printed on a clear background so that you can keep an eye on bathers even if they pull the curtain closed.

BATH MATS Look for one that's machine washable. If it doesn't have an anti-slip backing, keep it stationary by using a piece of the rubber anti-skid sheeting designed for area rugs.

KNOBS AND PULLS Decorating according to your child's interests or personality is simple with the variety of cabinet hardware available and the ease of installation. Replace knobs on vanities and cabinets with playful styles in a wide range of colors and finishes, and exchange them when your child outgrows the look.

A STURDY STOOL A good stool is an essential tool for any child's bathroom. It should have a wide, stable base with a large standing surface and be tall enough for your child to reach the sink faucet easily. An alternative

Black and white photos of vintage race cars give this sleek and sophisticated bath a unique twist.

Update bath cabinetry with novelty hardware from Lowe's. It can be replaced easily when the child outgrows the style.

ABOVE: The addition of a 12-inch-long kick-pleated ruffle and decorative trim takes this plain shower curtain to new heights.

This handy stool
complements the
clean, simple style
of the bath while
providing small
children a leg up
on toothbrushing.

is to hire a contractor to build a step into the sink vanity. Such a feature can be designed to fold down from the back of a door or slide out from the vanity like a drawer.

TOILET SEATS These are a cinch to replace. Pick a brightly colored one, and the entire bathroom instantly will feel more welcoming.

MIRROR If your child is unable to see himself in the mirror while standing on a stool, try adding an adjustable shaving mirror to the sink area.

HANDHELD SHOWER Consider swapping out your showerhead for a handheld model with a long hose. They are great for bathing young kids. Set it on a gentle spray, and it will allow you to rinse the shampoo out of a bather's hair without getting suds into sensitive eyes. An even more functional version of this convenience is the showerhead that slides along a vertical bar, making for easy height adjustment.

ABOVE AND BELOW: An assortment of themed bath accessories from Lowe's makes for foolproof decorating.

COUNTERTOP CONTAINERS When it comes to soap dishes and dispensers, toothbrush holders, and other sink-side containers, use non-breakable plastic instead of the standard ceramic options. You can find them in many fun colors.

WINDOW TREATMENTS It can be tempting to install plain window treatments in the damp environment of a child's bathroom, but making the right choice can add style as well as privacy to the space. Vinyl or faux-wood blinds are great options for moisture resistance, and these come in a variety of sizes and looks.

WALL ART Choose artwork that will appeal to your child and match the rest of the room's decor. Vintage advertising posters with images of kids are excellent picks. Or shoot a series of photographs of your child and frame the best of them for the bathroom wall.

GOOD CLEAN FUN

Use vinyl letters and numbers—already squared up for easy application—to embellish a vinyl shower curtain. Sketch out your plan on a piece of paper, using the curtain's dimensions as a guide. For inspiration you might consider names, descriptive words, or even your favorite quote. We used chrome curtain rings to accent the black and white graphic scheme against brightly colored walls. The letters and numbers are fairly inexpensive, so buy several packs and have fun.

Lowe's Shopping List

- vinyl letters
- vinyl numbers
- vinyl shower liner
- shower hooks

Skill level: Beginner
Rough cost estimate: $20
Rough time estimate: ½ day

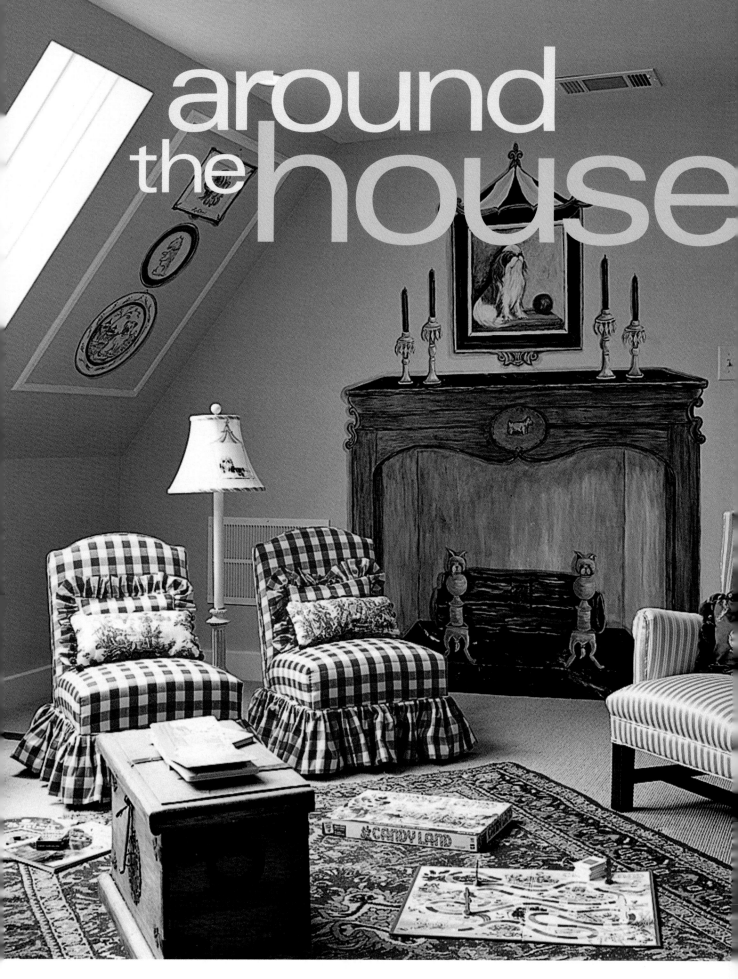

around the house

THE ARRIVAL OF KIDS CHANGES more than your lifestyle—it also transforms your home. The moment your newborn comes home from the hospital, items such as a play mat, a baby swing, and a diaper changing station begin to encroach upon your living space. Later, when your toddler takes his first steps, you may need to rearrange and redecorate to keep him out of trouble. And by the time one or more grade-schoolers are living in the house, games, toys, and gear can easily take over every square inch.

The good news is that you can still live in an attractive, tasteful home, even after children enter the picture. The following pages offer dozens of ways to create a stimulating and warm environment for youngsters—in all areas of the home, not just their bedrooms. A variety of clever storage options make play areas disappear when they are not in use. You'll also learn ways to maximize space, choose furniture that is both stain-resistant and sophisticated, and transform your children's artistic accomplishments and colorful toys into interior design assets. In addition, you will discover how to create inclusiveness in your home's shared spaces, so that family members can work and play alongside one another with ease.

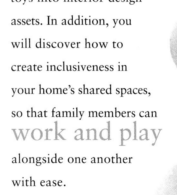

LEFT: Clever paint treatments, casual furniture, and durable yet fun accessories combine for a comfortable space that children can call their own.

planning the space

THE FOLLOWING PRINCIPLES will help transform common areas of your home into kid- and adult-friendly environments.

• Open floor plans work best for families because they create an inclusive, communal atmosphere. Parents are able to supervise their kids, and children feel more at ease being close to their parents, even if they are only one room away. Just removing the doors between kitchens, hallways, dining rooms, and living rooms will open up the space, enabling everyone to do their own activities while sharing a feeling of togetherness.

• Consider converting a formal dining room into a family-friendly space if your house is small and already has an eat-in-kitchen. Dining rooms typically are utilized for only a few holiday dinners, so it doesn't make sense to leave that square footage unused for the remainder of the year. Transform the formal dining room into a year-round playroom, a family room, or even an extra bedroom—with temporary dining solutions devised for crowds when needed.

• Establish clear rules about which rooms are only for adults. When your children are young, closed and locked doors or baby gates will set boundaries around home offices, formal living rooms, garages, or other spaces. Later, when they're old enough for supervised visits into these areas, remind them of the special rules that apply there.

• Remove all breakables from harm's way. Fine china, antique collectibles, and crystal figurines should be out of reach for young children. Consider relocating these fragile items to more formal rooms, cabinets with sturdy glass doors, high shelves, or long-term storage boxes.

RIGHT: This home's open floor plan makes it easy for an adult in the kitchen to supervise play in the den or homework at the dining table. A large ottoman provides a surface for board games as well as extra seating.

family rooms

EVERY HOME SHOULD HAVE A CASUAL SPACE where family members spend time together. While formal living rooms often display breakables or priceless antiques, a family room should provide everyday comfort with casual furnishings and low-maintenance finishes. In other words, televisions and sound systems make their homes alongside jigsaw puzzles, video game systems, and wooden blocks. Here are a few tips on how to create a space that's safe and comfortable for the whole family.

• To make the family room an inviting space for lounging on the floor, you'll need flooring that's either very soft or easily softened by accessories. The advantage of carpeting is that it can be wall-to-wall, but area rugs are a bit more stylish. Size your area rug so that it sits just in front of furnishings, and

RIGHT: Low, accessible shelving for toys and books; a big, soft rug for a comfortable lounge on the floor; a colorful, stain-hiding sofa; and soft ottomans that double as play surfaces make this a child-friendly family room. ABOVE: Storage close to the floor enables kids to pull out their toys more easily—and put them away again too.

ABOVE: Lots of soft seating facing the entertainment center ensures that family movie nights are enjoyable for everyone. The ottoman offers a perfect place to serve up snacks because it and the rest of the furniture have been stain-proofed. BELOW: A cozy haven for kids is simple to create by incorporating furniture with slipcovers, sturdy toy storage, colorful artwork, and a wide-open floor space for play.

place a thick carpet pad underneath to give it extra softness.

• Consider purchasing a round coffee table, or outfit corners with protective cushions. This part of your family room quickly will become your child's favorite play area and jungle gym, so keep in mind that the hard edges and corners of a traditional coffee table can be hazardous to toddlers. Or you might break with convention altogether and use a sturdy, oversized ottoman. It will supply a similar play surface for kids with plenty of cushioning. An ottoman also can double as a handy diaper-changing station if washable changing pads are stored nearby.

• Provide plenty of seating so that everyone in the family can enjoy the room together. For family movie nights that are comfortable for all, furniture should be angled toward the television. If you have small children, seating can be created out of something as simple as a bean bag or a pile of pillows on the floor. A soft rug or plush carpeting makes floor seating even cozier.

• Position stereo equipment and televisions inside a childproof entertainment center or armoire. This prevents the old sandwich-in-the-VCR-slot trick that kids love. It also takes youngsters' focus away from the television, so they enjoy more time doing

lively activities, such as playing games and cultivating hobbies.

• Offer shelving or storage that's accessible to the youngest members of the family. As in other rooms in the house, it's important for children to be able to reach their own toys and games and put them back up again. Large storage chests double as coffee tables and toy storage. Plastic containers filled with craft supplies can be stashed underneath skirted tables.

• Durable finishes are key in a room where children are going to spend much of their time. Just as brushed-metal faucets make for

ABOVE: This family room is kid-friendly and offers durable, low-maintenance tile flooring softened by a colorful rug from Lowe's. Plenty of space for game and media storage is accommodated by the entertainment center.

ADD-ON COMFORT

This spacious family room addition—in the former garage—is filled with places to play games, watch television, or read.

A NOOK provides ample common space for the family desk and computer.

A WINDOW SEAT creates additional seating while carpet topped with a soft area rug offers a comfortable lounging spot.

AMPLE STORAGE is found in baskets beneath tables, as well as in cabinetry under the window seat and in the office nook.

easy-to-clean bathroom vanities, accessories like machine-washable slipcovers or colorful fabrics go a long way in hiding dirt and safeguarding furniture. This multipurpose area attracts spills and other messes. So protect furnishings with stain-proofing to avoid permanent damage.

• Think about locating a shared computer in the family room. In this area, parents easily can monitor kids' Web browsing and limit time spent playing computer games. A central location also will make it possible for adults to do work on the computer while supervising youngsters at play.

Trend Update:

FAMILY ROOM

A family room addition is a great way to update an older home. Houses built before World War II—and the advent of television—often were designed without one. Adding this 21st century convenience doesn't require the plumbing or other costly features of a kitchen or a bathroom, so this type of addition can be a relatively low-cost job. One common approach is to build it directly off the kitchen, which can make a modest kitchen feel bigger, yield space for a dinette set, and provide an open floor plan between the two rooms that are used most in the house.

the family office

PARENTS OF CHILDREN WHO ARE OLD ENOUGH TO USE A COMPUTER FOR SCHOOLWORK—not to mention e-mail friends, play games, and eventually shop online—face a thoroughly modern parenting challenge: how to provide access to the Internet while protecting kids from inappropriate material. It's also important to regulate the amount of time spent playing computer games and sending "instant messages," and to make sure that they're keeping up with all of their homework.

A good solution is to create a family office in a spot that enables you to provide as much supervision as necessary. Put it in the corner of a den, a finished basement, the family room, or an existing home office. You can build it in a living room closet, on a large stair landing, or inside a freestanding armoire. The objective is to locate the space somewhere that allows you to keep an eye on the kids, until you decide they're old enough for a computer of their own. In the meantime, here are some more tips for creating a shared family office.

ABOVE: A roomy desk in this family room is great for homework as well as supervised computer time. Cabinetry adds storage space for games and school supplies.

• Choose a large desk, with plenty of space where kids can organize their projects. Extra storage space can be used to stock reference materials, such as age-appropriate dictionaries and a compact disc–based encyclopedia, as well as plenty of office supplies and arts-and-crafts materials.

• Try to locate the office away from distractions, such as televisions and playrooms.

• Accommodate individuals of different sizes at the same desk with an adjustable office chair. An additional comfy chair in the space will provide children with a place to curl up and read.

• Dedicate individual storage space—for virtual and hard-copy documents—for each family member. Personal electronic files can be stored on your computer's hard drive in folders named for each person. For hard copies, provide a segmented file drawer, plastic file box, or wall shelving.

• Protect your electronic files—such as family financial records and work-related documents—from accidental deletion by young computer-users. Use password protection for those programs and be vigilant about backing up your files.

• Adjust browser preferences to block inappropriate sites when your children are old enough to surf the Web. You also can track exactly where your child is going on the Internet by checking the browser's "history" or by using a "spy ware" program sold for this purpose.

before

after

playrooms

PLAYTIME IS A SIGNIFICANT PART OF BEING A KID, but the toys and activities take up a lot of space. So it's great to be able to dedicate one large area or room entirely to the pursuit. A finished basement or attic, a three-season porch, an extra room over the garage, or even an unused bedroom can be transformed into a playroom. In some cases, different rules may be established for this area than for the remainder of the house. Running, throwing lightweight balls, and blowing off steam may even be encouraged—especially when foul weather prevents children from enjoying the freedom of being outdoors.

A playroom can evolve along with your kids. In the early years, perhaps it's a toy room with plenty of floor space to spread out a vast wooden train set or play with a dollhouse. As they mature, it might become a "rec room," with game tables for playing pool, table tennis, or foosball, or an entertainment center for watching movies and playing video games. Someday, it might even provide a bedroom for a teenager in need of more privacy. Following are some tips for planning the space.

This "play" room, designed to suit the needs of older kids, has plenty of space for sports equipment and electronics. A backgammon paint treatment and game-oriented accessories create a backdrop for furniture upholstered with paint drop cloths.

RIGHT: A well-equipped beverage station can be squeezed into a small space. This one serves up a durable sink, an under-counter fridge, and cabinetry for snacks, glasses, and utensils.

LEFT: Set against the wall, this truck toolbox functions as storage area and a bench with a cool industrial look. A board painted red and blue is attached with wood screws to two stools, creating a coffee table that also serves as a large work surface.

Textured carpeting gives this attic playroom a finished look and is easy to keep clean.

Construction Details

If you're converting a basement, attic, garage space, or porch, take the opportunity to add features that will make your playroom efficient and practical.

BATHROOM It is true that adding a bathroom can increase construction costs. Nevertheless, it will aid youngsters who are learning to use the potty, provide facilities for your child's guests when the playroom later becomes a rec room, and possibly give your teenager her own bedroom suite if she moves into the space.

RECESSED LIGHTING Whether your ceiling is made from drywall or acoustical tiles, include plenty of recessed lighting. These fixtures sit flush with the ceiling, which makes for a clean design and reduces the chance they'll be damaged by active kids. Put in a grid of lights every 3 to 4 feet across the ceiling—with multiple dimming circuits—and the room will be bright enough for any task.

UTILITY SINK Somewhere in the space, build in a deep kitchen-style sink to make cleanup—of everything from snacks to painting projects—easy.

Kid-Friendly Finishes

When choosing surface materials for your playroom, the most important features are durability and hassle-free cleanup.

WALLS Solid-wood paneling will take a lot more abuse than wallboard, and without sustaining holes and dents. Another stylish alternative is to install a 3- or 4-foot-high beaded-board wainscot around the base of the walls. Use semigloss paint, which is easier to wash than a flat or eggshell finish. You also might consider installing wall panels below chair rails or in other scuff-prone areas.

FLOORS Wall-to-wall carpeting is the most comfortable underfoot, and commercial-grade versions are tough enough for busy playrooms. Still, you may get more longevity from resilient flooring such as vinyl, linoleum, or laminate—especially where moisture could become an issue, such as in a basement.

STAIRS Cover stairs and landings with carpeting. Make sure to provide sturdy banisters on each side of your staircase with balusters spaced no more than 4 inches apart. And consider adding an additional banister at a lower height to accommodate young children.

ABOVE: Durability and comfort combine in this pool house play space, with indoor/outdoor furniture, beaded-board paneling, and low-nap, stain-resistant carpet.

ABOVE AND RIGHT:
The sloped ceiling in this colorful attic room creates the illusion of a grand space, but the furniture is scaled just for kids. Low shelving units hold toys and books, and a small table provides room for art projects. Scrubbable flooring makes cleanup easy.

Furnishing the Playroom

A playroom is a place where the normal rules of decorating don't apply—what matters is durability, comfort, and effortless cleaning.

FURNITURE You don't have to buy new furnishings for a playroom. Instead, consider replacing sofas and other pieces in the living room or family room and moving the old items into the new play space. Machine-washable slipcovers are a good idea for protecting upholstered pieces. Another hardy, inexpensive way to furnish a room is with indoor/outdoor furniture.

CRAFTS AREA Provide a crafts area designed to accommodate the messes made by creative materials such as paint and glue. An old kitchen table can double as a crafts

<<< PUPPET THEATER

Aspiring puppeteers are sure to fall in love with this whimsical play area. With minimal materials, you can construct the perfect setting for productions. For a list of materials and instructions on how to complete this project, go to **Lowes.com/PuppetTheater**.

WHAT A GREAT IDEA

ABOVE: While its configuration would work equally well as a homework spot, this space in an attic playroom is outfitted for after-school snacks.

kitchens

THE KITCHEN IS THE HEART OF THE HOME. Adults tend to spend a lot of time cooking, eating, and socializing there. Family life will be much more inclusive if this is a place where youngsters can feel at ease and entertain themselves too.

OPEN LAYOUT A kitchen with an open floor plan is the best fit for a modern lifestyle. If the space borders a family room or other living area, your kids can play in one room while you cook in another. And, conversely, when your children are old enough to make their own lunches, you will be able to supervise from a close distance, without appearing too overbearing.

NEARBY PLAY ZONES Whether it is in an adjoining room or in the kitchen itself, provide an area where small children can play independently while you prepare a meal or clean up after one. A soft rug and a toy bucket may be all you need.

BREAKFAST BAR A high countertop that overhangs the cabinetry provides a bar-like surface where family members can enjoy a meal or snack in a more casual setting. It's also an ideal kitchen feature for a household with children. (An adjustable-height stool with a safety strap will bring a youngster up to the counter.) And sitting at the bar to eat, coloring with crayons, or just hanging out gives children the chance to observe the cooking process—and perhaps lend a hand. This is beneficial for curious kids who are not yet tall enough to see the food preparations from the floor.

SMART APPLIANCES Buttons, knobs, and levers really appeal to children. So look for kitchen equipment with controls that

RIGHT: This functional, well-lit space adjacent to the kitchen can serve as many things—a spot for planning menus and grocery lists, playing games (and keeping score), working on school projects, or eating dinner as a family.

The chalkboard contains the following handwritten notes:

eggs
Milk
Cookies
Juice
Soda
Olive Oil
Pasta
Sunscreen
green tea

MOM—
gone to
the
beach!

Jessy & Rose

Call
-Nancy
-John
-Michael
-Shelly

storage

KEEP LIVING SPACE FROM LOOKING LIKE A GYMNASIUM OR ROMPER ROOM by providing stylish storage areas throughout your home. Plan for your items to be located in a purposeful place, close to where you use them most.

MULTIPURPOSE STORAGE End tables that are actually hinged storage boxes, and coffee tables that have built-in drawers or cabinets, are good for stashing overflow items in high-traffic living rooms. Also, the cushions on many benches and ottomans lift up to reveal compartments underneath.

RIGHT AND ABOVE: In this wall of storage, tall units hold coats and sports uniforms, while interior shelves and hooks organize extra gear and household supplies. A nearby basket catches overflow. Waist-high units with drawers hold smaller items and provide a work surface. Message boards above keep the family informed.

To Do
* WRAP BI
* PACK FOR
* ARRANG
* GRADUATI

The ample cabinetry beneath this cozy window seat supplies extra storage space, offering lots of room for games or other overflow items.

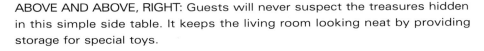

ABOVE AND ABOVE, RIGHT: Guests will never suspect the treasures hidden in this simple side table. It keeps the living room looking neat by providing storage for special toys.

BUILT-INS You can add lots of storage by hiring a contractor to construct built-in shelving, window seats with drawers, diner-style booths with space for odds and ends under the seats, or any number of other details with interior compartments.

TOY BOXES These are the workhorses in the category of toy storage, and every play area in the house can benefit from having one. Essentially lift-top chests, all toy boxes have one important feature: safety hinges that prevent the lid from slamming shut.

KIDS' CLOSETS If space permits, closets in the playroom and family room are ideal for warehousing toys and projects. Install shelves, or use a closet system to create shallow cubbies where youngsters can stow playthings behind closed doors.

STORAGE FURNITURE Create more toy storage throughout the house by giving kids access to specific drawers, cabinets, and cubbies inside sturdy pieces of furniture, such as armoires, bureaus, and hutches. Just remember to tether tall pieces to the wall to keep children from pulling them over.

KITCHEN CABINETS As a rule, kitchen cabinets should be secured with childproof latches, but consider leaving a couple of cabinets or drawers unlatched and loading them with safe, well-organized toys.

LONG-TERM STORAGE SECRETS

A great way to keep an organized attic, basement, and garage is to buy lots of large plastic containers with snap-tight lids. When it is time to put something away—from holiday decorations to off-season clothing to outgrown toys that await the next child—stow them in a container with like items. Use a label maker to identify exactly what is inside, stick the label on the side of the container, and stack it in the storage area with the label facing outward. Your belongings will stay clean and bug-free, and they'll be easy to find later.

cubby organizer

HOW TO: build it

Wherever your storage challenges exist, this project will solve them. The cubby holds and sorts toys, gardening supplies, or sports equipment for tonight's practice. Seal it suitably for indoor or outdoor use, and it will last a long time.

TOOL LIST

- miter saw
- saber saw
- circular saw
- drill with bits
- paintbrush
- framing square
- tape measure
- pencil
- sanding sponge
- hammer

Lowe's Shopping List

Lumber

- 2 (6-foot-long) 1 x 12 (#2) pine boards
- 1 (12-foot-long) 1 x 6 (#2) pine board
- 1 (10-foot-long) 1 x 6 (#2) pine board
- 1 (6-foot-long) 1 x 6 (#2) pine board
- 1 (6-foot-long) 1 x 2 (#2) pine board
- 1 ($^{13}\!/_{64}$-inch-thick) 48- x 32-inch piece of unfinished oak wainscot

Assembly/Finishing Materials

- either 1 box 6d hot-dipped galvanized finishing nails OR 1 box 2½-inch PrimeGuard Plus exterior screws
- 1 (8-ounce) bottle Titebond II Premium Wood Glue
- 1 box 4d galvanized exterior box nails
- paint or stain
- clear polyurethane

GENERAL: Assemble all parts using 6d nails or exterior screws, except where noted, predrilling and countersinking. Glue joints first; remove excess with a damp cloth. Patch holes with wood putty, and sand. **Remember to sand all pieces before assembling them.**

STEP 1: Cut all pieces per the Cutting Diagram and Cut List, except for the stringers and dividers.

STEP 2: Lay out and cut the stringers, as shown in Figure 1. Lay out and cut the upper, middle, and lower dividers, as shown in Figures 2 and 3.

STEP 3: Attach the top and bottom to the stringers. Check for square.

STEP 4: Connect the cleat at the top back corner of each stringer.

STEP 5: Secure the back panel to the top, bottom, and stringers with 4d nails. Check for square before nailing.

STEP 6: Attach the shelves per the layout lines, as shown in Figure 1, or set the cubby on its back and dry-fit the shelves and dividers. This will show where to fasten the shelves to the stringers and provide a check that the dividers are cut correctly.

STEP 7: Install the dividers per the layout lines shown in Figure 4. Check for square to shelf. Because the dividers are in line, you cannot fasten into the top and bottom of all of the dividers. Start with the lower dividers, and fasten from the bottom board and from the bottom shelf down. Attach the bottom outside lip. (These are the only dividers that can be fastened from the top and bottom.) Fasten the middle dividers from the top shelf down, then attach middle outside lip. Fasten the upper dividers from the top down, then attach the upper outside lip. Attaching the outside lips as you go makes it easier to fasten the dividers. Also, fastening through the lips provides a second fastening point, increasing the stability of the dividers.

STEP 8: Mark nailing lines for the shelves and dividers on the back panel. Nail with 4d box nails. Then nail with 6d nails or insert exterior screws through the

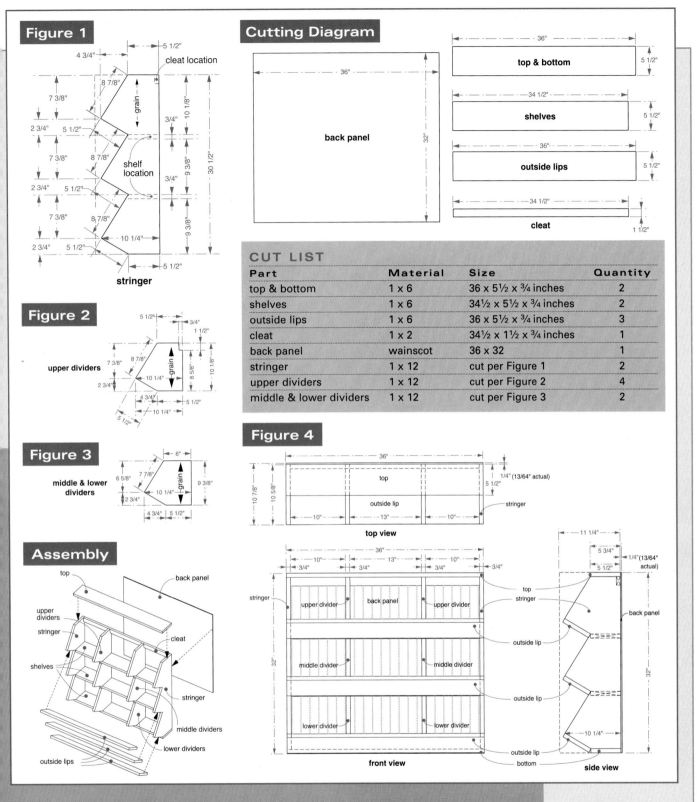

Figure 1

cleat location

stringer

Figure 2

upper dividers

Figure 3

middle & lower dividers

Cutting Diagram

back panel

top & bottom

shelves

outside lips

cleat

CUT LIST

Part	Material	Size	Quantity
top & bottom	1 x 6	36 x 5½ x ¾ inches	2
shelves	1 x 6	34½ x 5½ x ¾ inches	2
outside lips	1 x 6	36 x 5½ x ¾ inches	3
cleat	1 x 2	34½ x 1½ x ¾ inches	1
back panel	wainscot	36 x 32	1
stringer	1 x 12	cut per Figure 1	2
upper dividers	1 x 12	cut per Figure 2	4
middle & lower dividers	1 x 12	cut per Figure 3	2

Figure 4

top view

front view

side view

Assembly

top of the back panel, through the cleat, and into the upper dividers to strengthen the cleat attachment. If the unit is to hold heavy items, add another cleat along the back panel's bottom edge.

STEP 9: Ease the edges by hand sanding with a sponge sanding block. Sand the unit to desired smoothness.

Apply multiple coats of exterior latex paint, or stain and coat with clear polyurethane to desired finish.

STEP 10: Predrill to attach the cubby to the wall, and then drive appropriately sized screws through the cleat into the wall studs.

outdoor
spaces

Watching over playtime is simplified when the structure is placed within view of a window, deck, or patio. Parents can comfortably keep an eye on children playing in this backyard.

SOME KIDS EMBRACE THE OUTDOORS, while others are less eager to play outside. But once they're in the midst of nature, most children are reluctant to come back indoors. In the yard, they can run, yell, jump, dig, swing, and even climb. They can spray each other with the hose and invent many other delightful ways to make grass-stained, muddy messes of themselves. In the process, they learn about the natural world while gaining physical skills, such as throwing a ball, riding a bicycle, and turning a cartwheel.

They can perform all of these activities in just about any yard—from a small lot to a sprawling property. Still, there are ways that you can ratchet up the fun. Plant a garden that abounds with appealing colors, scents, and edibles, for example. Or fill your landscape with plants that will attract butterflies and hummingbirds. Best of all, some high-quality play equipment will yield hours of healthful amusement. Pick a shady spot that's within easy sight of the house for your choice of apparatus, which may be anything from a sandbox to a multilevel play structure. The area should be surrounded by a fence or a thick hedge of shrubs to create an enclosure for play. Then supply plenty of toys and games, and you have a multifaceted backyard that will both entertain and tire out your active kids better than anything they do indoors.

planning the space

IT ONLY TAKES A FEW PIECES of equipment to transform an ordinary backyard into a thrilling playground. But what is best for your play area depends on your property, your kids, and your budget.

CLIMBING Inexpensive plastic climbers and slides will suffice for little tykes. But by the time they're in grade school, kids really need something tall, solid, and sturdy. Look for modular equipment that can be expanded or altered as your children grow. For instance, you can select a combination of age-appropriate swings, rope ladders, monkey bars, rock-climbing walls, or spiral-tube slides, and then change the components later. To construct the unit, either cedar or redwood is the best option. Be sure that you use, at a minimum, 4 x 4 posts and 2 x 6 swing beams.

BELOW: Belted swings are great for kids once they outgrow the toddler swing. Plastic-coated chains keep small hands from getting pinched.

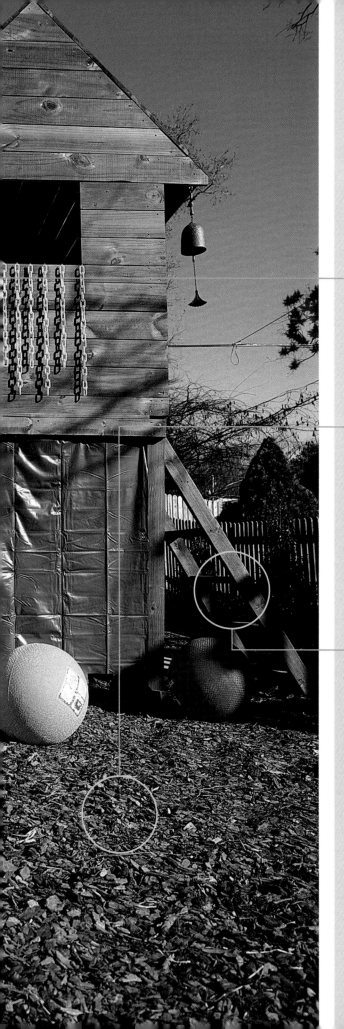

PLAYGROUND SAFETY

Nearly 50,000 children are injured in backyard playgrounds each year, so it's vital that parents follow some safety precautions.

• **INSTALL GUARDRAILS** on all decks, porches, stairs, climber platforms, and ramps. They should have balusters that are spaced no more than $2\frac{3}{8}$ inches apart.

• **PROVIDE A SHOCK-ABSORBENT SURFACE**—a 9-inch-deep layer of wood chips, mulch, or shredded rubber—at least 6 feet in all directions around play equipment. For swings, the surface should extend out from the swing beam (the member supporting the swing) by at least twice the height of the bar. (Note the proper mulch depth on the climber posts with an indelible marker to make easy work of restoring the mulch in the future.) You also can lay rubber tiles or poured-in-place rubber surfaces designed for this purpose.

• **REMOVE OR BURY TRIPPING HAZARDS,** such as tree stumps, exposed roots, rocks, and concrete footings.

• **RUNGS SHOULD BE AT LEAST** 9 inches apart to prevent children from getting trapped.

• **USE A TODDLER SWING** with a side, back, and three-point harness until your child is at least 3 years old. They are available in a variety of fun, colorful designs. Your child is ready for a regular swing when her feet touch the ground while she's sitting in it and she's strong enough to hold herself in place.

An outbuilding or shed can be transformed into the playhouse of her dreams. This one from Lowe's was painted and given a tin roof to create a cute cottage style. A simple deck provides the shed with a sound footing and an outdoor extension.

PLAYHOUSES You can purchase lightweight plastic versions, assemble-it-yourself kits made of wood, or prefab wooden playhouses that are dressed up with everything from front porches to fancy Victorian mouldings. When selecting a large playhouse, think about how well its shape and size can be repurposed for something else, such as a lawn-tool shed, when the children outgrow it.

TREE HOUSES Perched high above the yard, a tree house quickly will become your kids' favorite hangout. A grouping of three or four healthy, mature trees spaced evenly apart can serve as posts for the elevated structure. Or, hire a contractor or specialty tree-house builder who can construct the entire building from the support of a single tree. The lag screws used to attach the house should

Consider the following kid-friendly features for your outside play spaces.

• **AN AREA OF FLAT, LEVEL LAWN** provides a site for every outdoor activity, from playing ball on the weekend to pitching a tent for a backyard camp-out. If your yard contains a steep grade, consider hiring a landscape contractor to level the entire area or a portion of it.

• **A PATIO OR DECK** offers a spot to sit and watch the children play, as well as an alfresco family eating area. If it's at ground level, the patio is often the best surface for riding wheeled toys.

• **AN OUTDOOR "PLAYROOM"** prevents children's belongings from overtaking the yard, just as a playroom in the house segregates toys from other indoor spaces. Pick a shady spot that's easily viewed from your house and use a line of small shrubs, a stone wall, or some symbolic barrier to divide the area from the rest of the yard. Then fill the space with play gear—and places to store it.

• **SPORTS EQUIPMENT** that can be put away after each use, such as horseshoes, collapsible basketball hoops, portable soccer goals, and volleyball nets, will help to limit yard clutter.

• **A CHILDREN'S GARDEN** will provide your young ones with a unique opportunity to learn about nature. Not only will they develop their green thumbs, but they also may discover a lifelong hobby.

not harm a healthy, mature tree, but you also could have the structure built with supports from the ground. As a rule of thumb, anchor the tree house at no higher than one-eighth of the tree height. And make sure to provide the appropriate railings, along with a safe and sturdy ladder that's fixed in place.

SPLASH FEATURES   The simple childhood joy of running through the sprinkler has been taken to a new level with the introduction of decorative sprinklers that can be attached to garden hoses. These colorful metal

sculptures come in a wide range of styles, such as water cannons shaped like blowfish, serpents that spit jets of water, and buckets perched high above the ground that gradually fill with water and then dump a giant bath onto little heads.

SWIMMING POOLS   Not long ago, you had to settle for a shallow plastic kiddie pool if you didn't have the yard space or the budget for a full-scale, permanent one. But a whole new breed of pools is now available on the market. These temporary above-ground pools consist of inflatable

walls made of heavy-duty rubber. They come in sizes from 2 to 4 feet deep and 8 to 24 feet in diameter. Equipped with filters, chlorinated water, pumps, and skimmers, they can remain in place all summer long. And for only $100 to $700, the price is right. Requirements for pool installation are simple: flat level ground to locate it and an outdoor power supply to plug in the pump. However, you also may need to add a fence (see "Pool Fences" on page 125). If you live in an area where the pool will be closed for the off-season, be sure to use a cover that's strong enough to support the weight of a young child, just in case.

SKATE RAMPS Perhaps the trendiest of all backyard equipment, skate ramps bear a resemblance to a large pipe divided in half. They allow skate boarders, bike riders, and in-line skaters to test their inner daredevils. You can purchase these contraptions from a specialty retailer, or you may choose to build your own. Just make certain that your child always wears proper head, elbow, and knee protection.

RIGHT: The addition of casters to this sandbox makes it easy to roll in- or outdoors for play or storage. A shelf underneath holds buckets and shovels, while the handy lid keeps sand clean and relatively dry. The lid also provides a play surface when the kids tire of the sand. The cedar planks were spaced slightly apart so that water could drain through. For materials and instructions on building this project, log on to LowesCreativeIdeas.com.

SANDBOX BASICS

Perhaps no single backyard feature will provide more hours of focused play than the classic sandbox. Create a basic model that's fun, clean, and safe.

• SAND SHOULD BE AT LEAST 12 INCHES DEEP so that children can dig without reaching bottom. (Double that depth is even better.) The simplest way to construct the sides is to cut cedar boards between 2 x 8 and 2 x 12 feet in size. Screw the boards together and set them in a hole that has been cut exactly to the footprint of the sandbox.

• SANDBOXES WITHOUT SOLID BOTTOMS ARE BEST, because water needs to be able to drain through the sand. A bottomless sandbox installed in the ground will allow rain to wash the sand, while preventing water from puddling and spilling over the sides, which could lead to mold growth. Excavate to the desirable sand depth—taking into account the height of the walls—then install and level the box and fill it with sand. For an above-ground sandbox (like the one shown at left), gaps between the planks will allow water to drain.

• SAND IS SOLD BY THE CUBIC YARD. (One cubic yard equals 27 cubic feet.) So divide the cubic feet by 27 to determine how many cubic yards to order, and then round the number up. For example, a sandbox that measures 4 x 8 feet and is 2 feet deep will need about 2½ cubic yards of sand (4 x 8 x 2 = 64; $^{64}/_{27}$ = 2.37 cubic yards).

FROM SPORTING GEAR to sandbox trucks, kids' stuff can take over your yard. The items also can incur weather damage and harm the grass underneath. Thus, it is essential to provide places conducive to stowing outdoor belongings. If you have either a walk-out basement or a garage that is convenient to the backyard, use a closet or a large storage cabinet located just inside the door. Otherwise, some outdoor storage will need to be added.

GEAR ORGANIZERS If you have space indoors, these handy contraptions are built to hold all the bells and whistles that accompany the games kids love to play. For instance, mesh bags, bins, and concave shelves are all great for runaway basketballs, soccer balls, and the like. Other organizers offer a slotted shelf perfect for controlling things such as hockey sticks and baseball bats. Most of these systems tuck easily into the corner of a garage or carport.

DECK BUILT-INS Consider incorporating built-in storage if you are building a deck or have one that is alterable. Use decking materials to construct cabinets under bench seats, staircases, or the deck itself, if it stands 3 feet or more above ground.

SHEDS Although they are typically sold for storing items such as lawnmowers, pool cleaning equipment, and gardening tools, outdoor utility sheds can be terrific storage solutions for toys too. A simple utilitarian shed made of metal or wood might appeal to you. Or you may opt for a more playful design (similar to the one shown below): a wood-sided shed that resembles a house, complete with a peaked roof, glass windows, and plenty of charm.

LEFT: Customized garden sheds offer an attractive means of storing toys and other outdoor gear.

PLASTIC BINS Available in a variety of shapes and sizes, lightweight plastic containers are the simplest, most flexible, and least expensive storage solution. Be certain to select one with a lid that snaps on tightly so that it won't blow off in the wind. Also, if the bin doesn't have holes in the bottom, use a drill to make a few. This allows any water that does manage to get into the bin to drain out.

DECK BOXES Heavy-duty storage boxes are typically sold for storing garden tools and barbecue supplies, but they make great outdoor toy chests as well. However, they are not designed to be mobile. Because these deck boxes will damage any grass they sit on for long periods of time, it is best to locate them on a patio, deck, or mulch bed. Again, drill drainage holes in the base of the boxes if necessary.

ABOVE: These gear organizers make toy-strewn driveways a thing of the past. Slots, shelves, and bins keep balls, bats, and other sports equipment contained and orderly.

GARDENING IS A WONDERFUL HOBBY FOR CHILDREN. It involves digging dirt and sprinkling water, which are two extraordinarily enjoyable activities for kids of any age. Furthermore, they can watch their gardens grow throughout the season, anticipate the vegetables or flowers that will be produced, and learn many powerful lessons about nature along the way. Following are some tips for gardening with youngsters.

• **Keep your children's garden small,** and plan to do most of the weeding and watering yourself.

• **Build a small container garden as an introduction to gardening for kids.** Locate it in a convenient spot, such as by the back door, and water it with an indoor watering can. If you use sterile potting soil, little, if any, weeding will be necessary. Low-maintenance, colorful annuals, such as impatiens, pansies, and petunias, are available in a rainbow of colors. They will bloom profusely all summer long if spent flowers are deadheaded regularly.

• **Plant something from seed with your child.** Watching a seed turn into a full-grown plant is a truly miraculous experience, especially for young children. Some excellent plants that can be sown in the ground include basil, sunflowers, and ornamental gourds.

• **Create a themed garden.** A pizza garden filled with tomatoes, peppers, and oregano is ideal for a July cooking project. Or choose plants with interesting aromas—such as

ABOVE: These raised beds—one for each sibling— were planted with herbs, vegetables, and flowers. RIGHT: Success belongs to both hardworking children, with each bed producing above and beyond their expectations.

LEFT: Starting from scratch is easy with these kid-friendly seed kits. The mini-greenhouses come with several seed varieties, including herbs, flowers, and succulents. Help your child start a kit in a sunny window.

scented geraniums (available with a variety of scents, from chocolate to cinnamon)—around your yard. A garden also can be personalized with a bed shaped like the first initial of your little one's name or with plants that bloom in her favorite color.

• **Help your child select a specimen tree or shrub for your yard.** She'll enjoy selecting a place of honor for it where she can watch it grow for years to come.

• **Assist an older child in planting a perennial garden just outside her bedroom window or another favorite outdoor spot.** Since this garden will be visible throughout the year, it is important to select a grouping of plants that will provide color during every season: bulbs in spring, perennials in summer, colored foliage in fall, and dried seedpods and fruit in winter.

• **Design areas that attract wildlife.** The blossoms on coneflower and butterfly bush, for example, will attract butterflies. Blooms in salmon, pink, and crimson often lure hummingbirds to the garden. And birdfeeders can supply hours of entertainment as native birds flock to your yard.

ABOVE: This sunflower kit contains three seeds along with a peat pellet and container.

When the seedlings are big enough, according to the kit's instructions, transfer them to a large pot or to a plot outdoors.

birdingbliss

hummingbird feeder

WITH HELP FROM WILDLIFE EXPERTS, Lowe's has developed an exclusive line of products for birds that includes everything from feeders to houses to seeds. These items will make it easy for your family to enjoy backyard bird watching.

BIRD WATCHING & FEEDING TIPS

• Keep binoculars close by in order to view birds at a distance.

• Don't sleep in. Most birds are active in the morning.

• Learn which birds are common to your area, so you'll know when you spot a rare species.

• Offer feeders and seeds in an assortment of varieties and sizes to attract different kinds of birds.

• Keep your feeder clean and seeds dry. And store feed in an airtight metal canister to protect it from the elements, as well as from insects and rodents.

Napa wild bird feeder

watering can project

Let your child customize her own watering can.

"Gardening involves digging dirt and sprinkling water, which are two extraordinarily enjoyable activities for kids of any age."

HOW TO:

Wipe a metal watering can with mineral spirits before painting it. Spray it with metal primer, and then apply a base coat. (Make sure the nozzle does not become clogged

paint it

with paint.) Once it's dry, your child may paint designs of her own or apply rub-on transfers. After everything dries again, apply an even coat of Polycrylic to seal the exterior of the can.

MOSQUITO CONTROL

If you live in an area that is affected by the West Nile Virus, you need to be extra vigilant about protecting your kids from mosquito bites. These insects breed in standing water, so dump out nonchlorinated kiddie pools after use, store toys and gear where they won't collect rainwater, and eliminate any other places where water can collect and become stagnant, such as misaligned gutters or driveway potholes. Also, change the water in birdbaths weekly, and drill drainage holes in swings.

PROTECTING YOUR CHILD

Mosquitoes are most prevalent at dusk and dawn, so keep kids indoors during these times. And whenever they go outside, apply an insect repellent that contains deet. This chemical is the only one proven to repel mosquitoes, but it should be used with some precautions. To apply, place some in your hands and then rub it onto any exposed skin, as well as clothing and hair. Do not apply it to cuts or scrapes—or to hands, which are likely to touch their mouths. Once inside, children should bathe and change their clothes.

TREATING THE SPACE

Several products, called inhibitors, treat large spaces. Some dispel mosquitoes, while others attract and trap them—and some do either. Most manufacturers advise placing these machines about 50 feet from decks and patios, in areas that tend to attract mosquitos, such as those with dense foliage.

RIGHT: The Mosquito Deleto™ System by Coleman can be set to either attract and trap mosquitos or repel those that venture into your yard.

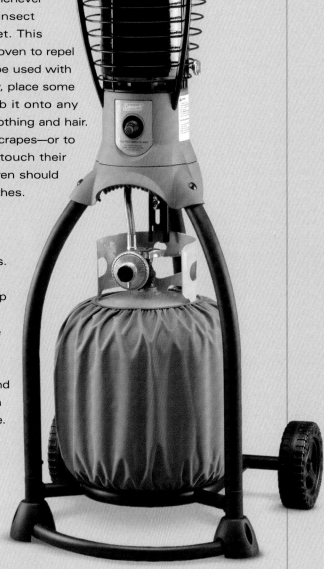

THERE'S AN OLD PROVERB that says, "Good fences make good neighbors," because they grant privacy to residents on both sides. Well, good fences also make good—not to mention safe—kids. They keep youngsters from wandering away and protect them from dangers such as busy streets and unfriendly neighborhood dogs. If you're in the market for a fence, you'll want to choose the right one for the job.

CONTAINMENT FENCES A 3- to 4-foot-high fence should be sufficient if you need to keep young children away from a danger, such as traffic or a steep slope, or if you just want to prevent them from leaving the yard. Spaced pickets and rail fences (the kind used for horse pastures) are traditional choices. In either case, openings should be no larger than 4 inches to prevent little ones from climbing through the gaps.

FRONT YARD FENCES Unless your house is located on a very busy intersection, it is preferable to keep front yard fencing low and open. An attractive rail fence, such as the one shown at right, will demarcate your property and contain your kids within the yard while maintaining a welcoming and neighborly appearance. Again, spaced pickets and rail fences with gaps of 4 inches or less and heights of 3- to 4-feet should be sufficient.

PRIVACY FENCES If your goal is to create a visual barrier so that your family can enjoy playing in the backyard without sharing the experience with the rest of the neighborhood, you will need a fence that provides a solid screen. Essentially, this means placing the pickets and boards (or vertical members of the fence) together so that there's

RIGHT: Along the borders of a front yard, where privacy may be less of an issue, an ornamental fence such as this one keeps young children, as well as stray basketballs, from finding their way into the street.

A hedge of evergreen trees behind a crisp white picket fence provides privacy and keeps games from spilling into the neighbors' yards.

ABOVE: This vinyl fence provides a degree of privacy as well as style, with the lattice border along the top. The absence of gaps between or under panels keeps the yard relatively secure, while a gate that's visible from several points within the house makes it easier for parents to monitor comings and goings. BELOW: A variety of evergreen shrubs and plants shield this home from the noise and sight of nearby traffic.

virtually no space between them. Or, to allow just a little light and air through, arrange for a slight gap (perhaps a half inch or 1 inch) between the boards. You also may opt for a lattice—a clever way to add ornamentation while still attaining the degree of privacy that you desire.

SECURITY FENCES In order to prevent passersby from wandering onto your property, a fence ideally will be 6 to 8 feet high. (Some towns restrict fence heights, so check with your local zoning department.) To impede someone from climbing over, the fence should have either a very narrow top or sharp pickets. Also, make sure it doesn't have footholds on the outside.

POOL FENCES Building codes in most states call for a 4- to 5-foot-tall pool fence that has a self-latching gate. In some cases, the fence must surround the pool area, while in others, it can wrap around the whole yard. Check with your local building department for more information.

LIVING FENCES Plants also can be used to create fences that safeguard kids and ensure privacy. Evergreens will provide coverage in all seasons, and ones that grow a thick mass of foliage will offer the most effective barrier. Privets, boxwoods, cypress, spruce, and yews are all good options. And some forms of holly have such tough, spiky leaves that they virtually eliminate the chance of anyone cutting through your hedge. For a more colorful living fence, consider a line of rhododendrons, forsythia, lilac, or ornamental grasses. Speak with your Lowe's Live Nursery Sales Specialist for specific recommendations of plants that will grow well in your yard and supply the kind of height you need. And don't be afraid to select multiple plant varieties—they will only create a more eye-catching hedge. To ensure that kids can not cut through a living fence, especially before it's fully grown, you can install a green wire fence right next to the shrubs and let stems and foliage grow through, over, and around it.

INDEX

Page numbers in **boldface** refer to photographs.

Adolescents. *See* Preteens and teens
Allergies or asthma, 42
Appliances, child-safe, 96, 98, **99**
Armoires, **24-25, 28,** 29, 85
Artwork display, 32, **32,** 49, **49,** 51, 72, **78, 82**
Attic spaces, **21, 61, 89, 93**

Babies. *See* Nursery; Safety
Bathroom
    extra touches, 62, **63,** 66, **67,** 68, **68, 69,** 70, **70,** 72, **72**
    faucets, **55,** 57
    fixtures (*See* Bathtub; Shower; Sinks)
    flooring, 56, **56**
    in the playroom, 89
    knobs and pulls, 64, **64,** 70, **70**
    lighting, 58, **58, 59**
    planning your, 54
    safety, 55, 57
    shared, 60, 61, **60-63,** 62, 63, **69**
    storage, **52, 61, 62,** 66-68, **66-69**
    towel racks, **55,** 62, 64, 66, **66,** 68, **68**
    vent fan, 58, 60
Bathtub, 54, 55, **56,** 57
Bedroom
    accessories, 9, **17, 22-23,** 39, 48-51, **48-51**
    activity zones in the, 10, 34-37, **34-37**
    changes as your child grows, 22-23, **22-23,** 44-45
    clothing and closet space, 26, **27,** 28-29, **28-31,** 31
    collectibles and displays, 32-33, **32-33**
    for preteens and teens, 16-17, **16, 17**
    for toddlers, 12-15, **12-15**
    headboard project, 46-47, **46-47**
    nurseries, 8-11, **8-11, 24, 28,** 51
    planning your, 12, 14, 48, 51
    shared, 18, **18-21,** 21
    storage, 24-27, **24-27**
Beds
    bunk, 21, **21**
    headboard project, 46-47, **46-47**
    junior-sized, 44
    storage under, **27**
    trundle, **18**
Beverage station, **88, 93**
Birds and birdfeeders, 120, 121, **121**
Breakfast bar, 96, **98**

Cabinetry
    bathroom, 66, **66, 69,** 70
    child-proofing the, 79, **79**

entryway, 100, **100**
for a computer workstation, **85**
for multipurpose storage, **104**
kitchen, 105
Card art project, 49, **49**
Carpeting, 42-43, **42-43,** 78, 91, **91**
Ceiling treatments, 38, 51
Chalkboard project, 95, **95**
Children
    bathroom fixture dimensions, 54, **55**
    changes as they grow, 22-23, **22-23,** 44-45
    decorating choices by, 12, 21
    eye-level measurements, 15
    furniture dimensions, 44
    shelving dimensions, 15
    supervising the, 76, 78, 84, 85, 96, **108-109,** 113
    weeding out possessions, 26
Closets
    bedroom, 26, **27,** 28-29, **28-31,** 31
    linen, **66, 67,** 68
    playroom or family room, 105
    shelving systems for, 26, **27,** **29-31**
Coat rack, 100, **100**
Collectibles, 32-33, **32-33,** 49, **49,** 51
Colors
    changes as your child grows, 22
    for preteens and teens, **16**
    nursery, **8-9,** 10
    planning the, 38, 41
Computer area, 35, 84, **84,** 85, **85**
Crafts area, 36, **36-37,** 78, 92, **92-93,** 94. *See also* Play areas
Cubbies
    bedroom, **18,** 29, 31
    entryway, 100
    family room, **80**
    how to build, 106-107, **106-107**

Deck boxes, 117
Deck built-ins, 116
Decorating sets, 48
Desks, 34, **34-35,** 85
Diaper-changing station, **8, 24,** 82
Dining room, 78, 96, **96-97**

Eating areas or stations, **88, 93,** 94, 96, **98, 99**
Entryway, 100, **100-101**
Ergonomic environment, 35

Family room, 80, **80-85,** 82-84
Fences, 124-125, **124-125**

Floor plan, open, 76, **76-77,** 84, 96, **96-97**
Flooring. *See also* Carpeting; Tile
    around the house, 78
    bathroom, 56, **56**
    bedroom, 23, 36, 42-43, **42-43**
    family room, 80, 82, **83**
    for stairs, 91
    playroom, **88-89, 90-91,** 91
Footstool, 54, **65,** 70, **71,** 98
Furniture
    armoires, **24-25, 28,** 29, 85
    bedroom, **44,** 44-45, **45**
    bunk beds, 21, **21**
    changes as your child grows, 22, **22-23**
    desks, 34, **34-35,** 85
    entryway, 100, **100-101**
    family room, 80, **80-81,** 83
    junior-size beds, 44
    modular, 44-45
    nursery, 8, **8-9,** 11, **24, 28**
    play area, **36**
    playroom, **88, 90-91,** 92, **92-93**
    shared bedrooms, **19**
    storage within, 105
    tables, 78, **92-93,** 98, **98**
    toddler's room, **12**

Garden, 113, 118, **118-123,** 120-123
Garden project, 122-123, **122-123**
Ground fault circuit interrupter (GFCI), 55
Growth chart project, 50, **50**

Hamper, 31
Headboard project, 46-47, **46-47**
Home entertainment centers, **24-25,** 83, **83**

Infants. *See* Nursery; Safety

Junior suite, 63, **63**
Junior-sized furniture, 44

Kitchen, 96, **96-99,** 98-99
Kitchen, make-believe, 94, **94**

Ladders, 21, **110-111**, 111
Landscaping plants as fences, 125, **125**
Laundry area, 67
Lead in paint, 39
Lighting
    bathroom, 58, **58**, **59**
    bedroom, **17**, 21, **21**, 45
    changes as your child grows, **22-23**
    computer workstation, 35
    for artwork display, **78**
    ideas to upgrade, 45
    playroom, 89
    task-oriented, 45, 78
    with bunk beds, 21, **21**

m

Magnet project, 34, **34**
Modular furniture, 44-45
Mosquito control, 123
Mud room, 100
Mulch for play area, 111
Murals, **11**, **12-13**

n

Nursery, 8-11, **8-11**, **24**, **28**, **51**

o

Office area, 85, **85**. *See also* Computer
    area
Outdoor space
    fences, 124-125, **124-125**
    garden, 113, 118, **118-123**, 120-123
    mosquito control, 123
    planning your, 110-115
    storage, **116**, 116-117, **117**
    supervising the children, **108-109**,
        113

p

Paint
    playroom, 90
    safety, 39
    shopping tips, 38, 41
Pesticides, 123
Planning
    bathroom, 54, 64
    changes as your child grows, 22-23,
        22-23, 44
    colors, 38, 41
    nursery, 10
    outdoor spaces, 110-115
    your child-friendly home, 76, 78
Play areas. *See also* Sports equipment;
    Toys
    bedroom, 34, **34**, 36, **36-37**
    family room, 78, **82**
    kitchen, 78, 96, 98
    outdoor, 113
Play structures, outdoor, 110, **110-111**

Playhouses, 112, **112-113**
Playroom, 86, **86-95**, 89-92, 94-95
Preteens and teens
    bedroom, **16**, 16-17, **17**
    computer area, 35, 84, **84**, 85, **85**
    junior suite, 63, **63**
    playroom, 86, **86-89**, 89
    refrigerator toys for, 98
Projects
    card art, 49, **49**
    chalkboard, 95, **95**
    cubby organizer, 106-107, **106-107**
    display ideas, 32, **32**
    growth chart, 50, **50**
    headboard, 46-47, **46-47**
    magnet, 34, **34**
    shower curtain, **72-73**, 73
    wall stripes, 40, **40**
    watering can, 122-123, **122-123**
Puppet theater, 93, **93**

r

Refrigerator toys, 98

s

Safety
    allergies or asthma and carpeting,
        42
    bunk beds, 21
    child-proofing the house, 11, 27,
        43, 55, 76, 79, **79**
    in outdoor play areas, **110-111**,111
    in the bathroom, 55, 57
    in the kitchen, 98, **99**
    light bulbs, 45
    mosquito control, 123
    paint, 39
Sand, 115
Sandbox, 114, **114**, 115, **115**
Shared spaces
    bathroom, 60, **60-63**, 62, 63, **69**
    bedroom, 18, **18-21**, 21
    garden, **118**, 119
Shed, 116, **116**
Shelving systems, 26, **27**, **29-31**
Shower, **56**, 57, 61, **61**, 64, 72
Shower caddy, 66
Shower curtain project, **72-73**, 73
Sinks, **52**, 58, 60, **65**, **88**, 89
Skate ramp, 114
Slides, **110**
Smoke detectors, 99, **99**
Splash features, 113
Sports equipment, 86, 94, **102**, 113,
    116, **116**, **117**
Stairs, 79, 91
Storage
    bathroom, **52**, **61**, **62**, 66-68, **66-69**
    bedroom, 24-27, **24-27**
    closet systems for, 26, **27-31**
    family room, **80**, 83
    for computer accessories, 85
    for toys
        bathroom, 66, **69**
        bedroom, 18, 26, **27**, **29**, **33**
        family room, **80**, 83

    within furniture, 105, **105**
    long-term, 105
    multipurpose, 102, **102-105**,104
    outdoor, **116**, 116-117, **117**
    playroom, 92
Study areas, 16, 34, **34**, 35, **35**
Swimming pools, 113-114, 125
Swings, 110, **110**, 111, **111**

t

Tables, 78, **92-93**, 98, **98**
Teenagers. *See* Preteens and teens
Television and media areas, **24-25**, 83, **83**
Thermostat settings
    for nursery, 10
    for water heater, 55
Tile
    in the bathroom, 56, **56**, 58
    rubber, 34, 36, 43
Toddlers, 12-15, **12-15**. *See also* Safety
Toys, 34, **34**, 98. *See also* Play areas;
    Playroom; Storage
Tree houses, 112-113

u

Universal Design, 10, 64

v

Vent fan, 58, 60

w

Wainscot, 38, **38**, 58
Wall treatments
    designs, **14-15**, **86-87**
    in the playroom, **86-87**, 90
    murals, **11**, **12-13**
    privacy in the bathroom, 60
    stripes, **6-7**, **39**, 40, **40**, **51**
    wainscot, 38, **38**, 58
    wallpaper, 38, **38**
Water features, 113
Water heater, 55, 60
Watering can project, 122-123, **122-123**
Web browsing, 85
Weeding your possessions, 26
Wheelchair accessibility, 64, **65**, 78
Window nook, **10**, **26**, **27**, **36**, **84-85**,
    104
Window treatments, 10, **10**, **11**, **27**,
    43, 72

AT LOWE'S...
we're here for you!

Because of our commitment to customer service, Lowe's has expanded its offerings to help homeowners complete their renovations and projects. Here are the top 10 ways in which Lowe's can help you with your home improvement endeavors.

1 Professionals install. Upgrades such as flooring, plumbing fixtures, and cabinetry require knowledge and time. Lowe's can provide guaranteed professional installation.

2 Just ask us, and we'll order it. Take advantage of our Special Order Services. With access to more than 250,000 products, you're bound to find whatever item you're seeking.

3 We offer payment options. Take a look at Lowe's Consumer Credit Card as an option to finance your next project. Apply by visiting Lowes.com and clicking "Credit," or simply drop by the store nearest you for an application.

4 We assist. We deliver, and we can provide guaranteed professional installation.

5 We match your colors. Bring a sample to Lowe's, and our computers will create a matching paint shade in minutes.

6 We guarantee our prices. Our everyday low-price guarantee eliminates comparison shopping. If we find an identical item priced lower elsewhere, we will match the price. Should we happen to miss one, we will take off an additional 10%.

7 Our return policy is hassle free. If you are not completely happy with your purchase, simply return it, along with your original sales receipt, to any local Lowe's store within 90 days.* We'll either repair it, replace it, refund your money, or credit your account.

*30 days for outdoor power equipment (chain saws, blowers, tillers, trimmers, mowers, and pressure washers)

8 We offer friendly service. If you have any questions about a project, ask our knowledgeable staff. They'll be happy to find a solution within our store. Browse through additional projects at Lowes.com.

9 Our experts teach you how. Check out our free How-To Clinics on every subject from installing ceramic tile to organizing storage space. For more information and to sign up, visit your local Lowe's store, or go to Lowes.com/Clinics.

How-To CLINICS

10 We guarantee our plants. If a plant doesn't survive for a year after purchase, return it to your local store with the receipt, and we'll replace it.

1 YEAR GUARANTEE ON EVERY PLANT